The Dom's Guide to Tickling

by

Erik11

ISBN: **978-1-7339988-1-9**

Cover Illustrations by Achilles.

Acknowledgements

This book has been a labor of love for a very long time and to finally get it out to the public has been an incredible journey. It certainly takes a village to raise a child, and this manual has been in the infant stages for a very long time. Through the years I've been coaxed and cajoled to share tips and tricks. I'd write something and put it away. Write something else. Reorganize it. Rewrite it. It never seemed to reach a critical mass until this year. Finally, it's done. I am humbled and honored to have had the help and amazing support of my incredible cohorts.

I'd like pay homage to my friends and editors CB, and CJ. Each provided insight and commentary which helped make this book a more readable, usable resource.

Huge thanks to Furball for his modeling assistance, and Karl for letting me have enough of Furball's time to get the pictures right. And to my good friend Zac, the resident expert on mummification, without whom I'd have no mummification pictures.

I'd also like to thank Cat from Myfriendsfeet.com, who helped me connect with Achilles. And Achilles for his incredible artistic talent which helped make the book cover design really pop.

Lastly, I'd like to thank you, the reader. Without you, there would be no reason to share.   -

Erik11, 2019

Contents

Acknowledgements.....................................3

Tickling? 9

Consent 15

Safewords & Disclosures.........................26

The Parachute............................. 32

The Level Set 34

Disclosure Topics 35

Safe Sex Commentary 42

The Machete Factor 44

A Frame of Mind 46

To Tie or Not to Tie..................................61

The Shoelace Trick 67

Finally. Trust Established. Bondage
Time 70

Handcuffs 75

Restraints 78

Slings.......................................83

Stocks......................................85

Alternatives to Bed Bondage and
Other Thoughts.......................88

Blindfolding Your Submissive and Deprivation 96

Mummification 99

Where to Find Bondage Gear 106

The Erotic Theater................................ 108

The Coach 114

Frat House Hazing 116

The Spy...................................... 120

Peasant and the King.................. 123

Slave Instructions........................ 126

The Robber 128

The Job Seeker........................... 130

How to Throw a Tickle Party 132

ERIK11's Tickle Party Rules . 136

What Does SIR Want? 138

The Art of the Tickle 154

Neuro-Linguistic Programming (NLP)... 156

Tools of the Trade...................... 162

The Momentum of a Tickling Scene 183

Face Tickling............................... 196

Arm and Torso Tickling 204

Tickling the Lower Body 213

Tickling the Feet 221

Where to find the Tickle Tribe 229

Sites for Tickle Discussions 231

A Tip About Anonymous Connects
.... 235

Video Clip Sites 238

Gatherings 246

‒ Images ‒

Figure   1 – Thumb Tie 69
Figure   2 – Ankle Column Tie 71
Figure   3 – Wrist Column Tie 72
Figure   4 – Crotch Grab 73
Figure   5 – Thumb Cuffs 75
Figure   6 – Double Lock Cuffs 76
Figure   7 – Hinged Cuffs 77
Figure   8 – Dog Collar and Carabiner 79
Figure   9 – Fist Mitts 81
Figure 10 – Leg Spreader 82
Figure 11 – Man in Stockade 86
Figure 12 – Portal Dungeon Straps 92
Figure 13 – Portal Dungeon Straps on Door .93

Figure 14 – EMT Board 94

Figure 15 – Man on EMT Board..................... 94

Figure 16 – Mummified with Feet Exposed. 100

Figure 17 – Mummified with Gag 101

Figure 18 – Mummified for Tickling............. 103

Figure 19 – Massager with Prongs 169

Figure 20 – Guitar Finger Picks 170

Figure 21 – Riding Crop............................... 176

Figure 22 – Wartenberg Wheel.................... 178

Figure 23 – Ice on a Spoon.......................... 179

Tickling?

The rough daddy took the Sub and threw him to the ground; his spit strewn across the Sub's face. "Who the fuck said you could TALK, boy?" A dirty yard boot stamped down an inch from the Sub's head. The Sub could smell the sidewalk and a musky odor of something his master had stepped in. He pulled at his bonds, but his hands were securely locked in fist mitts. His sweaty hands were useless and driving him insane in the leather bags locked on them. The Sub had been waiting all week for the moment. He never knew what was coming. It excited and scared him. His master, once again, would be using him. But he had really fucked up. Really. This time. And the furrowed brow of his master and the way the hood and gag had been slapped on him, were only precursors to the torment that lay before him. Already the Sub was trembling…but not because there was pain. No, pain was easy. Pain was yielding but not releasing. And this…this would be worse. The winch came to life and the sound of the ropes being hoisted surprised the Sub, whose bound hands were pulled upward above him. His legs, already locked in a leg spreader, were useless…and the Sub was yanked to a standing position, hands locked high above him.

Then the master began. Slow, agonizingly slow strokes up and down the nude bound Sub. Light scratches along the stomach, in the armpits, in the inner thigh, along the back, behind the knees, in the ears, and at the nape of the Sub's neck, in his waist and groin. Soft touches mixed with hard sudden prods and spidering of fingers that would grab and pull and push and smooth. The tension was immediate and palatable.

The Sub tried to withhold…his body began to quiver uncontrollably…he wouldn't let it happen. It wasn't going to happen. But he couldn't get control and the next thing he knew he was laughing. Laughing as the master kneaded and worked his body. And the Sub grew hard. As he lost control and gave in to the laughter from the unstoppable tickling, his cock throbbed with excitement.   Wave after wave of erotic energy flooded him in spite of the involuntary reactions his body was

11

suffering to the teasing. He was horny and hard, but unable to focus as the tickling sensations made him feel a different part of his body. A sharp sting forced the Sub to cry out as his ass was snapped with a riding crop, and then the tickling continued. Hard and soft the afternoon came and went for the Sub…his screams of laughter heard by only one man. His man…

Read that story to ten men and you will get ten different reactions. Some laugh at its perceived simplicity. Others are amazed by the erotic response they have when they read it. Others declare boldly that "THEY aren't ticklish!!!" and if anyone tried to tickle them, there'd be a fight. Others break into a huge grin and adjust their cocks. Others dismiss it as stupid, and say they don't get it. I mean it's only tickling, right?

This book is for the people who want to

explore tickling and its erotic connections. It will contain stories of encounters, examples of tickling techniques and discussion of the basic elements of a tickling scene between two consenting adults. It will contain helpful hints and suggestions for things to heighten a tickling scene, and things about which to be careful. Additionally, it discusses elements of standard power exchange protocol, with tips and opinions I've formed over the years in what helps make a successful scene.

With 30 years of exploring tickling across the world, and having mastered over a thousand tickling and BDSM sessions, the comments herein represent a compendium of information that is passed between ticklers and considered fairly common knowledge by many within the tickle fetish community. It's a list of things that work, have worked, and will work to maximize the results of a session in which a man gets tickled (by one or many).

Note: I'm not representing a community. But in a world in which I get hit up 10 times a month by someone asking me if I could teach them how to Dom, or teach their lover how to tickle, I decided it was time to share my knowledge in a more formal fashion. This book is my effort to formalize my tickling knowledge for novices or Dom's looking to get advice on how to master the art of tickling.

Consent

In my years of attending International Mister
Leather (IML), Folsom Street Fair, Dore Alley,
Cleveland Leather Awareness week (CLAW),
Esprit de Corps, and a host of other
gatherings, I've always been amazed at the
visceral responses I get when asking a
stranger about tickling. In the fetish world
where climax isn't necessarily considered the
end goal, these adrenaline junkies, guys who
would let themselves be hung by the heels and
beaten with a rubber hose for the endorphin
rush, often run for the hills when you mention
tickling will be part of a scene.

I'm not into coercion. I'm not going to trick
anyone into bondage and then torture them.
And here's why. Most are already victims of a
strange form of rape. I know many will balk at
this notion. Tickling is just kid's play. It's
nothing. Actually, this is totally untrue. Tickling,
in my opinion, is one of the highest forms of
sublimation; it's control without pain. It's an
exploitation of parental programming at its

base.

It can be a challenge getting one's partner to submit to this kind of teasing. Over the years, I have spoken with hundreds of subs who all rejected play when they heard tickling was involved.   It made no sense. Why would men, whose sexual identities are comprised of sublimation and degradation of any form, reject erotic touch?

I thought back to my first real tickling scene, which didn't really start out as a tickling scene, but rather a bondage session between my boyfriend and me. He was handcuffed to a weight bench, hands cuffed beneath the bench, and as I tied his feet to the weight rack, I accidentally tickled the soles of his feet. Honestly. It was an accident.   He laughed in hysterics. And as more of a prank than anything I did it again. And again. There was a rush of excitement as I heard him plead for me to stop. It was control. He had lost control and was truly helpless…and he knew it. And I figured it out faster than you can imagine. Didn't take much coaxing…I was hard as a rock from the moment he had started begging me to stop with a gigantic smile plastered across his face. A few moments later when he figured out I wasn't stopping…HE grew hard. And as I touched him everywhere from balls to underarms and feet, we both connected with an erotic energy which we had each never before experienced. That afternoon was my very first tickling session… four hours of exploring his ticklishness, with both of us climaxing harder than we had ever cum. About once an hour we'd both reach a peak and WHAM - climax. I had never experienced a headier sexual power exchange. So simple. And encapsulated through human touch.

But my partner had grown more and more hard as I tickled him more and more to excess. It seemed the more control I took from him, the more his cock filled and strained. He liked to be dominated and loved role-playing and exchanges of power during sex. He liked an "edge" to his play and this fit the bill.

Because I knew my partner, and he knew me, there was no perceived danger. And his response to the tickling reaffirmed something I believe to this day; Tickling is included as part of the human experience for use during SEX. Researchers have done studies to try and determine the reason humans are ticklish and can find no connection to other functions within a person's existence.   They often postulate it could be part of the "fight or flight" reaction.   I think they might have missed the connection.

But why are we ticklish? Here's my take: When you are 6 months old your nerve endings are brand new. Your parents touch you and your new body is flooded with energy, and you laugh. It's a joyous thing. They do it again and again. It's intimate. It's total trust. It's enjoyable. It makes you happy. Your parents lovingly nibble on your toes. They tickle your belly. It's all about making the baby laugh. And a Pavlovian response develops that when you are touched that way, you laugh.   Then you get to be 7 or 8...other people start to touch you that way who aren't your parents. It's a non-consensual intimacy - akin to rape in a really odd way. So, you do what anyone does in a rape situation; you go to fight or flight. You kick, you punch, you get angry, you roll yourself into a fetal ball… and many spend their whole life reinforcing this behavior pattern. Often people boast of their ability to "block" this sensation. They say "they used to be ticklish", but now they have "learned to turn it off". Actually, they haven't blocked it; it's a nerve response - but I'll explore how we get past the mental clamp in other chapters.

After tickling man after man and seeing the sexual stimulation it elicits, there is no doubt in my mind that sex and tickling are linked. And if that is the case, then when we were children, and tickled by our playmates – there was LOTS of perceived danger. If sexual response is linked to tickling, then as young adults we were being flooded with feelings and emotions we were unable to comprehend, for which we had no context, and of course we recoiled. It's hard enough for a full-grown man to relax and allow himself uninhibited sexual play without mixing in the control component. But as children, we just knew that tickling was an incredible energy rush, and that we lost control when someone tickled us. Some lost control of their bladders, most weakened and lost the ability to fight back, and all laughed without consent. Most being victimized through the non-consensual stimulation that our siblings and relatives repeated over and over under the guise of innocent play.

It's the conditioning of that early childhood non-consensual act which causes people to consider tickling in a negative light. It's labeled something which must be prevented. Something to be avoided at all costs. Many carry this primal fear. Many train themselves to block the sensations. To apply a "mental clamp" to allowing themselves to be weakened. But the ticklishness is still there, and still a part of the sexual response. During intimate moments, when we allow ourselves to be stroked erotically, the ticklish sensations also bring arousal. Think about it…everywhere that many are ticklish are erogenous zones; ears, neck, armpits, nipple/rib area, lower tummy, testicles, anus, inner thighs and feet.

As tickling continues to emerge as the "light"

kink of the new millennium (and it IS growing in popularity in leaps and bounds on the Internet these days) we need to find a way to bridge the gap of the childhood terror to transcend this block.

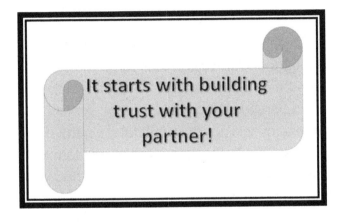

It starts with building trust with your partner!

When approaching the topic of a tickling session, ask your partner of their experiences in childhood. Talk about the helplessness it created in them and make them understand that as an adult, they can now choose to accept those erotic touches within the context they belong: as part of a consensual act of sex play. In much the same manner that maturing adults have to work at accepting anal stimulation, a powerfully erogenous zone they've been told was "dirty" their whole lives, it takes a mental deprogramming for most to engage comfortably with tickling. The mental clamp which they hold can easily be discarded by a submissive, when they trust.

For the fearful, tickle play needs to be incorporated in a slow, controlled fashion. Give your partner permission to laugh while you touch them. Spend an hour with them naked on the bed, touching them with the specific purpose of tickling. But don't take control from your partner. Tickle them, and allow them to laugh, and move unrestrained on the bed. Ask them where they were ticklish as a child, and then test each area. Ask them what works best as you determine the best area to tickle.

With new people, I often lay on top of them and have them hold me in a typical HUG position, with their arms wrapped around my body and then I gently tickle their sides while they laugh and squeeze me.

Go slow...help teach your partner that the ticklish sensations are positive ones; the laughter it brings from them is welcome, and encouraged. Phrases like "good boy" and "Let go and laugh" or "there ya go" or "that's it" should be whispered in their ear as you help them explore ticklish sensations in a safe environment. Make it positive and welcoming to laugh. Try and get them to not stifle the laughter. Tell them it's okay to laugh. Surprisingly many don't like the sound of their own laughter and will comment "I sound stupid when I laugh". Assure them you love everything about them and that their laugh will be great. It's best to use a rule of "no human words" when playing this way. Otherwise your partner may reduce the session to shouting for you to stop, instead of accepting and focusing on the tickling sensations. Set a time limit in which they can only laugh and hug you, and then keep to the agreed upon time. Set a timer for 2 minutes and then begin the lightly tease. Then switch to intimacy…you'll find that tickling your partner this way will create an intense amount of energy. They will get an endorphin rush from the exercise. Answer this rush with kissing, hugging, groping and other erotic elements of sex play which are not tickling.

The hardest part for the top in this groundwork is to remember that now is NOT the time to test your partner's limits for extended tickling. Don't pin them down and tickle rape them...there will be plenty of time for that once you have gotten them freely laughing, and have built some positive experiences.   If you push your partner and tickle to excess, you will reinforce that tickling is negative.   Make it fun. Sometimes trading off tickles is a great way to build this. Trade who gets to tickle and who is being tickled. Yes, even a Dom can be vulnerable for their partner. It's a gift you can offer your partner for good behavior!

Later chapters will describe techniques for tickling. If it were me...I'd have them shirtless, and run my fingertips lightly up and down their sides, while I lay on top of them. I might nuzzle or lick the base of their ear at the same time. And without a doubt, they would laugh. Once trust is established, and tickling is non-threatening and consensual, an amazing thing happens. Your partner will become aroused sexually. That partner who once cringed and got angry when tickled will actually enjoy the intimacy it implies. This is the essence of the tickle fetish. This is part of what we call "training". You are training your partner that tickling isn't negative, it's fun, results in incredible endorphin rush, and is about the safest form of play one could have.

Safewords & Disclosures

*The Sub had been laughing for 45 minutes. His body had long since sagged against the bondage. The winch that held him aloft and the fist mitts were no longer even noticeable to him. His legs were spread wide with the spreader bar and the master roughly fingered his hole. His firm dimpled butt cheeks were parted with expert fingers, and a feather was used to tickle the soft sensitive opening of his ass. The Sub, still laughing, cried out "NO, STOP....DON'T...STOP!!!"...it was more of a response than a request and mixed with the intense laughter, there was no cohesion to the comments...
the master continued playing...working the Sub into a fevered frenzy by alternating the tickling of his ribs while*

continuing to tease the Sub's hole. The master pushed the Sub, increasing the level of tickling, and the Sub's voice now filled the room with screams of laughter. Suddenly he shouted "BABYDOLL!" The master immediately stopped what he was doing and backed up.

The Sub hung for a second gasping for breath. Moments passed. He heaved and dropped into the bondage, allowing his full weight to fall. The Sub hung from his hands; all strength gone without hopes of returning. And although his cock was still rock hard. Still oozing precum. He seemed to have a look of fear on his face from a moment of panic that now was fading. Slowly his breath returned to a normal pace. And then he was ashamed. Ashamed he had

> *taken control back from the Dom.*
>
> *The master remained motionless, and waited for the Sub to gain his wits. Effectively, control had been returned…The Master asked the Sub if he was okay and wanted to continue, or if he had gotten to his limit and wanted to stop. The Sub, not really wanting to end everything nodded, asserting he wanted to go on, and the tickling continued…*

As stated before, tickling in the context of this manual is consensual. And when players are having a scene, often it's hard to distinguish in the throes of passion if your partner really means "stop" when he shouts it while his cock is rock hard and oozing precum. A safeword is the key. This is a special word which has been agreed upon by both players BEFORE any activity has occurred.   It's part of the negotiation of this kind of sexual congress. Woe be to he who does not clarify limits, boundaries and safewords <u>before</u> engaging in control drama with a dominant sexual partner. The submissive would be subject to the whim of the top with no way to signal that a boundary has been passed….be it physical, emotional, or intellectual. A safeword should be present every time you are engaging in a situation in which control is given. Even if you know your sexual partner well. Even if you have a good sense of confidence that your partner would never violate your wishes while helpless. When a Dominant guy is wound up, excited, and playing with you is not the time to suddenly decide you don't want some part of the scene. Often a submissive is gagged which prevents communication. A good dominant is watching and attuned to what's going on with their partner. A good dominant will check in with their partner to make sure they are okay. But many aren't good dominants.

The safeword should be a something which will NEVER come up in a scene between two partners. In our story, "BABYDOLL" is a word that would never have been part of the scene between the two players.

The word could be anything. The only requirement is that it is prearranged, it is easily distinguishable, and it can't be confused with something that might be said or done as part of the scene.   Sometimes a submissive will say "how about I just say STOP?"   I highly discourage this, because often SUB/DOM play is mixed with role-play, and saying "stop" might not really mean "stop".

Rules of thumb for your safeword:

- Make it something Absurdist

- Make the submissive say it out loud before play begins.

- Make sure everyone agrees on what happens when the word is said! Discuss with your partner exactly what is supposed to happen when the safeword is used.

Safewords normally take one of two forms: The "Parachute" and the "Level Set".

The Parachute

The <u>PARACHUTE</u> is a word that ends action. Whether it is in total, or just for a second, there is an immediate halt. Total stop is the form of this I prefer to use…my thought being, if the submissive is going to lose their trust in my abilities to run the scene and take control back, then the scene is over. That sounds harsh, but let's put it another way - a safeword, when used as a parachute, means the submissive doesn't feel **safe**. Ergo the term. They need to get out and get to a safe space. When the safeword is used, all bondage is removed, and everything comes to a close. Normally the scene is done at that point. It's a "parachute" to safety. Tickling is done in levels that build upon each other. Personally, I want a submissive to sign up for the ride.   And if I do my job correctly, by the end its going to be incredible for both of us. If they can't take the intensity, that's great, and they can parachute out. It does take an effort to give this kind of trust. But that's the dynamic that earns this activity the title - "edge play". Others impose a thirty to sixty second break to the play when the parachute is used. It's all a matter of taste and mutual agreement. Also, remember nothing precludes discussion while the scene is ongoing. The submissive can talk all they like unless instructed otherwise or gagged - the best scenes involve a lot of conversation. So, in my scenes the parachute is the way to end it. And a safeword ending to a scene doesn't mean you never play with that partner again. It means the Dom has established a little more trust, will observe wishes, keep agreements, and honors mutual consent. Typically, in these circumstances, the next scene is even *better*.

The Level Set

The <u>LEVEL SET</u> is used to change the intensity or to drive the controlling partner to change things. I've seen colors used extensively for this. RED for "back off, too intense, stop", YELLOW for "Slow down, it's almost too intense", and GREEN for "Okay, I'm ready to resume". This allows the submissive to send a message to the controlling partner. With pain play it's essential, because the Dominant may not have a good idea of the pain/pleasure point for the submissive. Tickling is far more subtle....and allowing this kind of control with the bottom may ultimately prevent the scene from intensifying. Because the ticklee may use the safeword over and over again, preventing the Top from getting them hyper-sensitized. There is nothing more frustrating to a DOM than to have his SUB take control from him over and over again.

Disclosure Topics

Ultimately the idea is for the SUB to want to endure the erotic sensations being used during play. It's consensual. And a note to both parties:

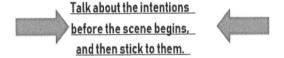

Talk about the intentions before the scene begins, and then stick to them.

What if a GAG is going to be used during the scene? A grunt code should be established. In my scenes I will have the submissive, during the negotiation phase at the beginning, grunt 5 short sharp grunts. This is their safeword when gagged.

Again, predetermine what the signal will be, and always agree upon one. When approaching sex in which control is being taken or given, coyness should be put aside and frank discussion should be had about the expectations of the scene before it occurs. Don't be shy about this. An experienced DOM should force the issue with the submissive and lead a discussion about how the scene will be handled. If the DOM doesn't, the SUB should definitely bring it up.   Tickling IS a form of control. And a scene in which someone is tickled is as serious as any other BDSM session in which someone is tied, spanked, whipped, milked, dildo'd, fucked, or any of a myriad of other sexual activities.

At a minimum, both parties should discuss the following:

- How long will the session last? Is the submissive signing up for the whole weekend? An hour? The afternoon? Until a specific time? Or until both parties are satisfied? (If you're a submissive, be careful when you agree to this, the DOM may take a whole day to climax…if the sub is lucky).

- What are the limits of the submissive (*things the submissive will not endure or will not allow)?* Examples might be: No rimming, No fluid exchange, no pain play, no scat, no water sports, no marks, No bruises, no animals, no fucking, no toys, no women, no children, nothing unsafe, no condoms, no use of Gorgonzola cheese…the point is the things that are not allowed are CLEARLY delineated.

- What is allowed? Gags? Hoods? Blindfolds? Bondage? Sounding? Electro Play? Hot wax? Spanking? Impact play? Isolation?

- Which kind of Safeword you will use and what happens when it is used?

- Any physical impairments the submissive has. Perhaps they have had broken bones in the past which makes some forms of bondage unachievable, or their current anal fissure prevents anal insertion. Perhaps they have psoriasis on their back and can't be whipped. It has to be discussed.

- Are either of the players involved with others (in "open" relationships), and what are the limits and constructs of those agreements. This is critical. I once had a guy tell me his partner wouldn't allow him to kiss anyone when they played with others. Unfortunately, I had to say no to playing with them, because for me, it's intimate and kissing is important. Of course, everyone has their own moral stance on these things and do as your conscience guides. Personally, I don't want to be the great sex that breaks up someone's marriage. But that's just me. Note: I WILL talk with someone's partner, if they claim there is an open relationship, and once the partner tells me the limits for their spouse I'll definitely play. But once again, this is me. I've been on the other side of a cheating partner, and I'd never voluntarily do this to another human. Karma is a bitch.

- Have either of the partners had a bad scene and what made it so? This is a really important topic, as it may give a submissive preconceived notion of things which might have only been the result of an inexperienced Dom or the misuse of new equipment.

- What is the general experience level of both

players? The last thing you want is to terrify that submissive who has only had one encounter, by taking him to some place they are not emotionally ready to experience. Ultimately, if you don't, the scene is likely to end quickly as the Submissive uses the safeword and rushes out the door. With time and experience, a good Dominant will watch the cues of their partner and know when things take the submissive out of "headspace".

- If it's an anonymous connection, what is the level of recognition you are allowed if you run into this person on the street? If you encounter this person at your best friend's next dinner party, are you allowed to acknowledge having met? When asked, most of my partners are curious that I even care. But an ounce of precaution will cure an evening of bad feelings or alienation when the wrong thing is said ... or NOT said. I side with being human with my encounters and greet people with whom I've been intimate in a friendly manner. Being a DOM means I provide the direction for what pleases me, but being a Man means putting it in a context that jives with reality. We have shared a trust, after all. But not everyone is like me. Men will lie for sex (imagine that) and Men will stretch the truth if it will gain them an orgasm. He could be married or partnered or even a clergyman. So, find out ahead of time what the rules of engagement should be if you happen to meet him at the confessional.

- Does the submissive have toys of their own they'd like you to use? I like to ask this question to my Subs, and they are always surprised and eager to offer up their favorite butt plug or dildo for my use on them. I make my submissives care for their own toys. They clean them, so they are sure what I'm using on them is sufficiently sterile to their needs. When we are done, they take them to the bathroom and wash them off. Besides being a great use of your submissive, it avoids having to spend extra money on rubbers for your dildo's and anti-bacterial soap/cleaner to clean them afterward.

- If it's a long scene (like over a weekend),

what are emergency numbers in case of…well…an emergency? This is really a hard one to get past. Many men approach fetish play with an air of anonymity, and when you begin asking questions like "what's your real name?" and "What is your phone number?" some men get queasy. If you are going to interact with someone for a weekend, you need to know what happens in an emergency. In 20 years, I've never had to resort to using this information but I've come extremely close. For extended play periods the DOM should at least ask how the submissive would like them to react if, say, the chain holding the sling breaks lose, the submissive falls, and cracks their head on the cement floor! Once they are passed out, is not the time to try and discern the right response.

Safe Sex Commentary

A word about safety: In today's day and age, in addition to HIV, it's important to make informed decisions to what one exposes oneself, and what they are willing to do. Safe sex is safe sex, and tickling is by far one of the safest forms of play one can encounter. There are pundits who claim, "if it's safe sex, why should I tell the other person my status? It's none of their business!" Accidents happen. Recently I met a man who was having safe sex and his partner ejaculated in his face. It was part of the scene, and they both had agreed it would be hot if the top ultimately brought himself off on the Bottoms face.   He got cum in the bottom's nose and eyes…both mucus membranes. Now my friend (the bottom) is HIV positive. He had only had sex with one guy that year…was negative prior, and knew conclusively this was the source of his infection. Yes, this was a remote possibility, and in 20 years of tickling scenes, there has never been a need for unsafe activity, nor has it come up much. Regardless, ask the question and make an informed choice. Paranoia isn't bad in these situations.   One unforeseen circumstance can change a life. Luckily with the advent of PrEP, there are options we can take to protect ourselves which weren't available 10 years ago and which don't necessarily predicate the use of condoms. And not to be controversial here, but if you can get other STD's orally (and all of the others you can), and you're not having your partner wear a condom when you engage in oral sex, then the ONLY thing that a condom really protects you from is HIV. PrEP will protect you with a 98% accuracy when taken as directed. That's a 2% possibility at serio-converting if you take a chance. Consider your risks wisely.

Normally, if you establish rules ahead of time, the worrisome factors of a scene can be mitigated. The Submissive should be at ease when the scene begins.

The Machete Factor

This is a term I coined a few years ago and it refers to a Dominant's first scene with a new Submissive. No matter what the Submissive's comfort level, no matter what has been said prior to the scene, or how well the Submissive knows the Dominant, the first time a submissive is dominated by a Dominant, they always expect the Dominant to break out a machete and hack them to pieces (in their primal mind). Regardless of what has transpired prior, know this to be true. The second time you play with someone there is much more trust and much more openness to simply "be in the moment". Dominant guys, please be aware of this – it's the difference between building trust and destroying possibility.

Safety, and the context for which it is protected within the scene sets the stage for extending the influence and effect of tickling. If the submissive ultimately trusts the dominant, it might get scary, but both parties are likely to have a fantastic time once the smoke clears and the tickling starts. With the disclosures out of the way and a safeword in place, the framework for how the play will be conducted has been established. If the submissive is scared of the control about to be taken – well, that's part of being a submissive. That's what's referred to as "an edge".   And Dom's should not misconstrue these disclosure steps as meaning they must give away every trick in their bag before they begin play. Surprise is key to a successful scene.   A Dom should cover the essentials (listed above) and keep the rest of the drama for the scene itself. Often submissives will ask question after question about what will happen; 'What toys will you use?', 'What will you do after I'm tied?', 'What happens after you tickle my feet?', etc. I shut this down quickly with a "You'll have to find out!" Don't budge on this point. It's very important that the elements of the scene be as spontaneous as possible. The Submissive will have a much better time if he has no preconceived notion and is completely surprised with each stroke the DOM makes.

A Frame of Mind

It had been a bad day for Frank. The batteries in his alarm clock had died sometime in the night and he had been late for work. His boss let him know his behavior was being watched; another late day and Frank would be let go. The day dragged on, and he barely gave a thought to what tonight was. It was the first evening of the full moon, and his master always required his presence at 7 PM sharp. Getting out of work, Frank looked at the sky and saw the wide circle of white light, realizing there was a long night ahead of him. On the way home, he stepped in dog crap, and twice people shoved him aside as he made his way to his brownstone apartment. He thought about the consequences of canceling on his master, but quickly dismissed that as a possibility. He cleaned himself out, shaved his face and pubes smooth, as his master required, donned his leather jockstrap and threw on street clothes. A 40-minute cab ride had him at his master's door with only 5 minutes to spare. He slipped off his shoes at the door, because that pleased his Master, and knocked.

The door opened.

"INSIDE Sub"

The master barked, and Frank tentatively entered. This was the third time they had seen each other, and each session was more incredible than the last. The room was darkened, and the glow of candles washed the house in softness. Music was playing, and the master stood, dressed in Jeans, chaps, black leather boots, and a chain link harness; his naked expansive chest perfectly framed by the metal chain.

Frank began trembling in excitement. This was going to be good. Again. The worries of the day melted into the resolve that he would need to make sure his master was pleased and to make sure his master was completely satisfied. He knew it was going to tickle... tickle really bad… but he was ready.

"SOCKS AND JOCK! NOW, Sub!!!"

*The master pointed at Frank;
his index finger directed at the
upper rib cage. "NOW!" he
ordered, poking Frank in the
ribs. Frank began lifting his
shirt to undress, but every time
he bared his chest raising the
cloth, the master would poke
him again. Frank pulled back
trying to avoid the contact, but
his master was on him with a
speed that could only be
brought on by a rush of sexual
excitement...light jab after light
jab prevented Frank from
removing his T shirt. Armpit,
stomach, armpit, stomach –
the master poked and prodded
Frank's torso. Finally, Frank
fell to the floor, as the Master
manhandled him down. The
master yanked Frank's shirt up
over his head, blinding Frank.
He held both of Frank's hands
above his head with a single
grip, the shirt blocking his
vision and tangling in his arms.
The master tickled him with his
free hand until Frank's giggling*

49

reached a fevered pitch. With the Master hovering over him, and Frank trapped on the floor underneath, there was no way Frank could escape. The master dropped his weight and straddled Frank's waist, further pinning him to the floor.

As always, Frank was helpless within seconds of entering the Master's home. Just the way he liked it…

Frank was into the scene. And it went from zero to sixty almost immediately. Authority was established, and the aggression of the Master truly provided the energy that kick started the scene.   Why do this? Because the Dominant wants the suggestion he is intimidating to be reinforced.

Often a submissive will test a dominant to see if they are willing to discipline them, or to put them into a situation in which they have no choice. If a Dom provides conditions for which the sub is to perform lest they get a "Correction", the Dom needs to stay with the program. If they say "you will say SIR after any time I speak, or you'll get that paddle" – then, if the Sub doesn't say "SIR", you paddle them. These kinds of constructs enforce authority, and provide a submissive who enjoys spanking a way to elicit the action.

Ultimately, it's about creating a setting in which both partners can play the roles that drive a satisfying sexual event. The Dom must make the first move, immediately establishing himself as the leader. The Master began the scene the moment the door opened. Since there had already been three sessions, no prep work was required for safewords and boundaries. The partners knew the limits and the rules. The Master knew Frank got off on being dominated, and in the past sessions (when he was handled aggressively) he became MORE ticklish. So, he immediately created an aggressive mood by giving Frank orders the moment he arrived.

In the story, Frank was told to wear a leather jock strap, and to shave certain parts of his body. The Master wore a harness that accented his physique. Each party wears what excites the other. It's part of setting the mood for the scene as well. If the Master came to the door wearing ballet slippers and a tutu, they might be able to still be dominant, but his submissive would be laughing at him from the moment they began. Dominants are authority figures, and whether leather gear is appealing, or whether jeans, t-shirt, and boots are desired, the important fact is visual cues are important in establishing the authoritarian stance. Think it's a coincidence that police officers wear sunglasses to shield their eyes? It's a trick to make them more intimidating. When policemen speak, they normally take a commanding tone…why? Because it reinforces that they hold authority. Often, I will hear a submissive complain that a previous scene in which they subbed was less than exciting. The Dom was half drunk. The television was blaring in the background. The dominant barely acted engaged while tying them up. There was no real structure. No beginning. No real end of any kind. The submissive never returned to them. Nor would I. If you were having vanilla sex, your partner would be engaged and focused. The same is required for role-play. It's still sex.

Power exchange play is a coordinated effort. The Dom has to work at creating the scene. The Submissive has to work at being what the Dom desires. Mind you, this doesn't mean that pretending the submissive is worthless might not be exciting, but remember…the bravest man in the room is the submissive. In general, the Dom should create the mood. It requires preparation and forethought. Will there be a negotiation beforehand? How will the Dom establish authority? What things do they require of the submissive? How should the submissive prepare?   A Dom should let a submissive know what kind of attire (or lack thereof) is expected of them. What time should they arrive? How long should they expect play to last? All of these should be established by the Dom and then the submissive needs to be told the elements for which he is responsible.

The Dom needs to make sure the setting for the scene lends itself to the kind of scene you are going to play. If couples are reading this book, and say "Well, how do I do this with my partner? He lives here…I can't create the mood after we just spent an evening together making dinner and cleaning dishes…" Actually, you can. It can be as easy as having the Submissive partner leave the house, and then ring the doorbell. This provides both a mental, as well as a physical beginning to the scene. Or send your partner to the store to buy duct tape and cling wrap. When he returns, the house is ready (and you now have the supplies for that mummification scene you've been wanting to try later in the week!) Never underestimate the importance of preparation during a tickle scene. Tickling has mental components as well as physical ones. That's why control games in which tickling is done are so interesting. The submissive must allow themselves to get to the point of hyper-sensitivity. Yes, the more tired a Sub is, the more ticklish he becomes, and wearing a Sub down is as good a method as any to increasing his ticklishness, but if you can get a submissive into the "Serving" mental groove (head-space) with a few tricks, why not do them? The more the Dom leads the way, the happier the Submissive is likely to be; a true submissive will revel in strong leadership.

In addition to the establishment of dominance, the surroundings should be as neutral as possible. Soft candle light or natural afternoon light makes for great sex play in general, and definitely for a nice tickle environment. Pitch black rooms can make for fun play as well in small doses; blindfolds serve the same purpose, and prevent the submissive from seeing toys (or anything for that matter). Some people opt for red lighting and satin sheets. The more intent that's placed on getting the mood established, the better the overall session.

The point is, did the Dominant think about it? Was it planned and executed? The DOM should have prepared an area for playing whether it be a wrestling mat on the floor (you can use a futon mattress for this as well) or a fully equipped bondage room with slings and stocks. All needed things should be at hand. Once a scene has begun, it will lose energy if a DOM is constantly looking for things, or stopping the action to locate that bottle of lube. Toys should be out of sight, but close at hand. "Everything is in control" is the mantra of the Master. Don't let that concept lose momentum during a scene. Once the play begins you want to build and build the intensity. Being prepared prevents boredom, and the Dom is responsible for making sure the submissive doesn't check out. There are many techniques for this, and it can be as simple as telling your sub to hold your riding crop in their teeth while you leave the room to keep them engaged. But the point is the Dom maintains the energy of the scene from beginning to end.

NOTE: Stopping play after a frenetic 30 minutes, for a 5-minute span of silence in which nothing is done can work a blinded submissive into a frenzy. He hears the Master leave the room, and has no idea what will happen next, or how long he will be waiting. It provides a setting in which anything can happen, and in which the submissive is reminded of their vulnerability. Even during this, a Master maintains control.

Choose music that enhances the mood. Ambient music or tribal music is always good. Make sure it's nothing to which your submissive can sing. You don't want them concentrating on that Judy Garland number when they should be focusing on the sensations to their body. Earlier I mentioned the "mental clamp" that people will develop to block their responses to tickling. This is one of their tricks – focusing the mind on something else. Remove music from becoming a hindrance to your tickling scene. I love foreign language chill music for this purpose. No one is going to be singing along to that French jazz album you have playing in the background. It absolutely needs to be something with a nice beat to which your sub **can't or won't sing along**.

All of this will add to the suggestibility of the scene. Yes. The *Suggestibility* of the scene. It's a seduction. Whatever levels the Sub plays at should be stoked when establishing the beginning of the scene. If the Submissive likes to be roughly undressed, make him wait for it to happen. Don't rush to the first action that entices him. Make him wait. Force him to hear the music playing. "NOSE TO THE RUG" is an order many of my Subs have heard over the years. It's normally the first moment of the scene, after they have removed their shoes. Ultimately, they will be naked. But as I said before, it's about building the momentum. This is how I create tension. I pinch their nipple. And then run my hands under their shirt. I continue prodding until I've found two to three ticklish spots. If he resists, I demand he strip to be tied. If he doesn't resist, then I continue tickling him until he does resist. Thus, escalating the attack and tickling until the Sub is consistently laughing. Either way, he's getting bound. But if it's an interaction, in which we both are engaged, sex gets quickly magnified from an energetic perspective. Many Dom's think it's not important for the Submissive to be turned on. And to each their own. I've found Submissives who are turned on are far more eager to comply. And in tickling, the submissive opens the door mentally. They unhinge the mental clamp. Once it's open (after the first scene and you've gotten them laughing), the frame of mind is set. But initial scenes are much better if you pace them and… control them.

Sometimes when meeting with a new Submissive, and talking limits, they smirk and roll their eyes. The uninitiated submissive doesn't understand the negotiation is required. Shocking them often will get them into head-space. Shocking them with the unexpected will fix this doubt. A trick I like is spitting water in their face. Something to startle them but that won't hurt them. Especially if you can surprise them with the action. Once again, it's about controlling the scene from beginning to end. A Dominant dominates, and the sooner you can show you're going to be a force with which they will have to reckon, the better. This is what the submissive wants. The Dominant will be controlling and forceful, if necessary. If they can't handle it, you'll hear the safeword. I've never had a guy safeword out with a wet face. Typically, they get hard and eager to be led.

I can already hear a chorus of voices of those reading this disagreeing. "I can tickle my Sub without needing his permission, and he's going to laugh!' True. Anyone can get raped. Once a Sub has been tickle trained, his sensitivity is constantly heightened. But with someone like Frank in our story, who has only played with this DOM three times, he needed a little comfort and setting to really lock him in. The Dom had music on, had dressed the part, and had lit candles. He took control immediately, and set the tone of the aggressive stance. Frank never had a moment to consider "can this guy really dominate me? " – and I can assure you, every Submissive who meets with a new Dom is wondering this from the beginning.

To Tie or Not to Tie

...that is the question.

Tony had wanted to meet with the master for many weeks. They had traded numerous emails, had chatted online, and finally had spoken on the phone. His fantasy had always been submitting to another man. Being put into a situation in which he had no choice, in which his options for backing out had been taken away. And yet...he really knew nothing of this man he had met online. TOPERIK's screen name implied fucking, but the profile that went with it spoke of "restraint, and the application of wood or other devices to the tender most parts of a body". The master seemed okay, and had assured Tony that if the scene became too intense, things would stop. But Tony didn't think he could give up that much control. On one hand the thought of losing control excited him, on the other it scared him. He could spend days with this person, but he knew that one day or 15 days would still not really give him enough information to fully trust this stranger. He had read accounts of people being victimized, and had talked about his fears with the master. Childhood had proved he had mild claustrophobia, and this would either reinforce that paranoia, or would dispel it.

His desire for sex was so strong, he went to the master's home, at the agreed upon time, and knocked on the door. The master was an *incredibly handsome man, mid 40's, frame well defined from years of gym work. He brought Tony into his home and offered him a beer. They talked, discussing safe words and limits. But when it came to the final scene, Tony couldn't allow himself to be tied. Something within his gut said "NO WAY", and he had to obey. Tony asked the master if they could just fuck, and was told unequivocally "No!" The Master explained the control turned him on, and there had to be elements of control taken or he wouldn't get sexually aroused. As a compromise, the Master asked if perhaps they could start with light bondage…maybe something simple? Tony, already fixed on not having any bondage, turned that down and finally, sadly, left.*

Amazingly enough, when conceptualizing play,

Submissives will romanticize the components of a scene in which control is given. Tony had an image in his head of how awesome it would be for someone to take control. But ultimately his claustrophobia got the better of him, and it became…. A boundary. This is honestly a difficult situation, and one that must be handled with extreme care. As a DOM, you really have no context to the submissive's psychological make up, and the human psyche is a minefield with emotional triggers which can take a sexual scene from ecstasy to horror in a flash. Presuming, because your SUB is willing to be stripped and flogged in public, that bondage won't be a challenge is very silly indeed. It's hard to give up control to someone. Movies like "PULP FICTION", and "CRUISING" link images of psychopaths and gay leather men. And often stereotypes are exactly that for a reason; because the object of the label really meets a consistent criterion. Why mention this? Because it's a Dom's job to do whatever they can to dispel the fear of giving up control, while still maintaining the air of authority. Not an easy task with a stranger. Should a DOM demand bondage? That depends on the

Master, and his reason for the requirement for that kind of control. Taking an inflexible stance as a DOM, without allowing for compromise will definitely limit your play. But as the Master in the story above, the Dom had specifically advertised restraints were going to be part of the scene, assuming he would compromise this desire was, honestly, an unrealistic expectation of the Submissive. The Dom in this scene isn't interested in the experience of the Submissive.

So, having said this, does a tickling session have to have bondage? Of course not. And many a wrestling match has been capped off with pinning and tickling an adversary. In this context, tickling is really introduced as a form of foreplay. Some tickling enthusiasts will allow themselves to be tickled without fighting. And for beginners, it's great to start without taking complete control from them. Earlier I discussed allowing your beginner partner to hug you, while you tickle his sides. He laughs, and hugs you tighter, but the rules are he cannot stop you in any way from tickling him anywhere you desire. The only downside with no bondage is receiving an elbow or knee in one's face as you lick your partner in that most sensitive area that results in uncontrollable "fight or flight" urges.

The Shoelace Trick

If you and your partner have played without
bondage for a while and you are looking to
ease into bondage, jumping to steel police
handcuffs may still intimidate the hell out of
your partner and be a bit advanced. Try this
trick. Use a shoelace and tie your partner's
thumbs together. Here's how: Place a barrier
between their hands and their body, like a bar
on a headboard, a column, a stair railing, or lay
them on a weight bench and tie their hands
UNDER the bench (while their body is above.)
Make a slip knot with one end of the lace, and
loop it over one thumb, pushing it all the way to
the webbing at the base of the thumb. Then
have your partner place their other thumb
against the first, thumb nails lined up, and loop
the shoelace around the base of the thumbs.
After about 8 loops, run the lace between the
two thumbs a few times. And you are done. No
need to tie anything off, and if the bottom tries
hard, with a little effort they can pull their
thumbs free.   When you are ready to really
restrain them, substitute a length of copper

wire for the shoelace, and your bottom will be as secure as it gets!

The point of the shoelace is to offer some resistance, but still allow them control. I'll tell you…the perceived control is pretty much an illusion. It's VERY hard to pull from this, but it's simple and most beginners are fine with this setup. Especially if you say "How about I tie you with just one of your shoelaces. It's more of a token than real bondage, and you'll be able to get out if you try, but we can pretend like you are really trapped."

Another position to use once their thumbs are tied is to crawl through the opening between their body and their arms, and use your body as the barrier. To do this, tie you partner's thumbs together in front of them and have them lay on the bed, hands above his head. Then straddle his waist and go in for a kiss. Have him lower his hands over your body as you pull your hands through. They are effectively pinned and you can tickle them on the ribs, underarms and sides, while simultaneously licking their neck…and unless you crawl out, they are stuck. This also works if the hands are cuffed, or even locked in to fist mitts.

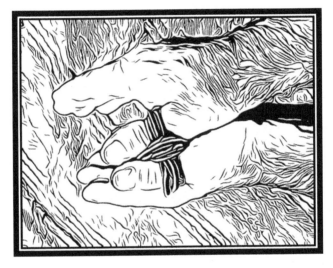

Figure 1 – Thumb Tie

Finally. Trust Established. Bondage Time

Once your partner is comfortable with bondage, there are many different configurations, as well as pieces of equipment that can be used for bondage with tickling. Many submissives love the feel of loops and loops of rope encircling them. The more loops, the more secure (typically). Loop someone's ankles a dozen times with rope, run the rope between the legs a few times, and tie it off, and your Submissive isn't going anywhere until you are ready.

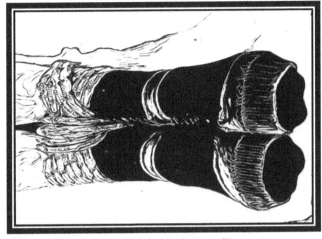

Figure 2 – Ankle Column Tie

It's the same with their wrists; a dozen loops
from wrist to elbow and back (arms in front,
palm to palm), looped a few times between the
arms, and tied off will not only prevent him
from moving his hands, but will reduce mobility
in his upper body.

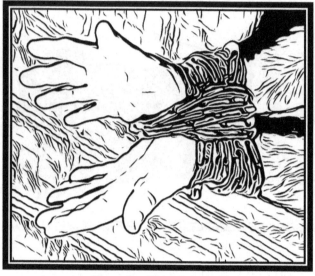

Figure 3 – Wrist Column Tie

Another looping trick is to loop rope above the knees 8 or 9 times and then slip it between the legs, and tie it off, and repeat the process just under the knee. This is particularly sneaky when your SUB is dressed. Jeans provide great padding (careful not to tie the loops so tight as to constrict blood circulation) and just enough resistance so you can reach between their legs, just below the fly and wiggle your fingertips. A light flutter of fingers inserted between the legs beneath the crotch will normally send a guy that's ticklish in that spot (and most are) into complete hysterics...and with the knees tied, and the hands restrained, there really is nothing they can do to stop you.

Figure 4 – Crotch Grab

Note that I say loop "A dozen" times, and "8 or 9 times." This is sincere, and compromising on the number of loops is affording your submissive the chance to wiggle free of bondage before you desire. This can really throw the pace of a scene off, as you then must stop to re-secure their bondage. On the positive side of this, should your SUB take the initiative to try and free themselves, I suggest 15 to 20 minutes of penalty tickling, once they are again secured. And don't mention this penalty until they ARE once again secured. Watch their face cloud with worry and dread at the thought of being put through those paces. And watch it light up as you begin tickling. But know this... bad bondage, of which a submissive can easily get themselves out, diminishes a scene. And remember the old adage... **"it's not bondage unless they want to get out,"** meaning, they can't get themselves out when they want to be out (that's what the safeword is for) otherwise it's secure.

Handcuffs

No Dom's bondage collection is complete without handcuffs, and many submissives like the feel of cold steel locked against their flesh. Handcuffs come in many sizes and shapes! There are thumb cuffs, which exploit the exact same physiological vulnerability on which the shoelace trick depends, locking the thumbs together at the base. They are small, easily transportable and have an air of innocence about them.

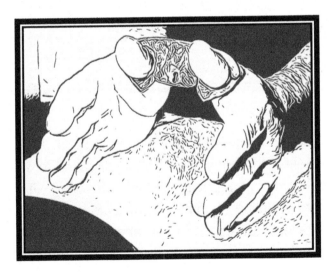

Figure 5 – Thumb Cuffs

Regulation handcuffs are the type with which most people are familiar, but even those have a wide variety of styles and shapes. When getting handcuffs, be sure to get a style that has an additional lock to prevent the cuffs from tightening once they are affixed to a wrist; these are called Double-Lock cuffs.

Figure 6 – Double Lock Cuffs

My favorite type of cuff is the hinged cuff. Their benefit is that they allow no mobility, and force the wrists into a position. Handcuffs bring with them a feeling of complete futility for the SUB's situation. But also, can hurt and cut when a submissive pulls against them. Talk about this with your Submissive before deciding to cuff them and tickle them to excess. They can really wind up with horrible marks and a few days' worth of soreness. All that said, some submissives are wild for the feel of metal encircling their limbs, putting them in a state of complete vulnerability, with only their master to depend on for their release.

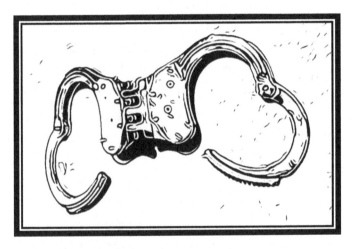

Figure 7 – Hinged Cuffs

Restraints

If handcuffs aren't your desire, or you seek
something with less bite, the roster of available
restraints is far and wide. Most are made of
leather, neoprene or plastic, and are shaped to
encase some or all of a limb, body, or head.
There are Hospital restraints, which normally
come in pairs; made specifically for either
wrists or ankles. They range in width from 1
inch to 4 inches, and normally have slits in one
end of the restraint, and a "D" ring in the other.
They are padded, and provide a nice, secure
bond. Since they are used with Hospital
patients normally, they are made for
professionals by professionals, and tend to be
highly effective. I use mine in combination with
spring steel Carabiner clips and dog collars. I
use the dog collars to fasten to the head board
and foot-board. Then attach one end of the
spring clip to the "D" ring the collar has for the
dog tag, and then fasten the spring clip to the
restraint's D ring.

Figure 8 – Dog Collar and Carabiner

This is secure, comfortable for the Sub, and easily removable should the need occur. Some restraints also add Velcro or a buckle and these are my favorites, as I can put them on my Sub and continue to change configurations of his bondage without having to take them off. Additionally, they are easily removed should something emergency occur which requires a scene to be shut down.

At a minimum, you should make sure you have something for securing the four points (wrists and ankles).

I personally couldn't survive without my fist mitts. These are like boxing gloves with no thumbs, and can be purchased from any serious bondage store. They are typically leather and completely encase the hand. There are many styles. The first is a standard puppy mitt with a Velcro close and a buckle, the second is a hospital version, which is a webbed glove with foam sewn into the palm. The fingertips poke out of these restraints, but the hands are useless. Another is a solid leather tube, with a rubber buckle at the wrist. I own some metal fist mitts that literally lock on a Sub's hand using an Allen wrench, and are extremely heavy. And another pair I own only encases 4 fingers on each hand, leaving the thumbs out. All are quite effective at making your Sub's hands completely irrelevant to the scene. Many Sub's love the challenge of escaping their bondage, and left to their own devices will revel in hours of Houdini play. Fist mitts make this not viable. Or rather, make using their hands for escape darn near impossible. Since they all buckle closed, there is no chance of thrashing or pulling tightening the bonds. Most that buckle also include a small metal post with a hole, making them "lockable" – a small padlock can be inserted making the leather buckle impossible to be opened until the lock is removed.

Figure 9 – Fist Mitts

If you are in a situation in which there seems to be nothing to which you can restrain your SUB's ankles, a leg spreader can be your solution. This device is an adjustable rod, with "D" rings on each end. Normally ankle restraints are tied to the ends of this, and the rod length is adjusted by the DOM. Forcing the legs wide. Sometimes I will tie a Sub's hands together, and then tie the hands to the bar of the leg spreader, face down. This forces their hands between their legs, and forces their legs wide open. The benefit is it exposes the Submissives soles and asshole. Just when they think they are going to get fucked, I start teasing their soles and drive them crazy.

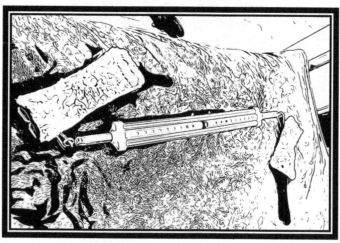

Figure 10 – Leg Spreader

Slings

Read a bondage magazine or hangout at your favorite sex club and you are sure to see a sling or two. Don't underestimate the use of a sling for tickling sessions.

Most slings are comprised of a rectangular leather swing seat, attached to 4 chains, which are hung from a ceiling or from a portable bondage rack. The leather seat hangs about waist high (this is to make it easier for the DOM to fuck his Sub in the sling). Most Subs are outfitted with ankle restraints and wrist restraints which are then affixed to the chains from the sling. The submissive is put on his back, on the leather swing. Normally the ankles are hung high, and the SUB is nude. The benefit of this is exposing the Sub's asshole; a VERY sensitive area. Additionally, the wiggle of the SUB will cause some swinging, but overall there is about 70% of the Submissive's body exposed. I've had subs tell me the swinging motion really gave them a surreal experience when hooded and placed

there. Add some tickling and I can assure your
SUB will truly know who the DOM is when it's
over.

One of the best scenes I've ever had with a
sling was with a guy that was hyper ticklish.
The slightest touch made this guy laugh and
thrash. I hung 15 feathers from strings from the
top of the sling. They were configured to just
barely touch him. He started thrashing from the
tickles which made the sling swing which made
the feathers move. Essentially, he tickled
himself to exhaustion over 15 minutes. I just
watched (videotaped).

Don't be afraid to use conventional bondage
equipment for tickling!

Stocks

Another favored bondage device is a solid set of stocks. In the upcoming chapter on Erotic Theater I mention the 'King and Peasant' scene, which makes use of them extensively. Stocks are highly effective at separating and restraining the soles of the feet for tickling. They normally are comprised of two wooden boards with half circles in each piece. The lower piece is affixed to a board and mounted. The second piece is normally hinged vertically, and closes over the ankles once they have been placed in the half circles of the lower half. More expensive kinds will include two additional smaller circles for wrists. Be sure to insulate the circles with towels, socks, padded leather, etc. because SUB's will pull and thrash against the tickling. A number of ticklers take their stocks a step further and place nails along the top of the stockade, which are then used to tie toes. If you want to see a guy with ticklish feet freak, put him in stocks, then tie his toes with shoelaces from his toes to the top of the stock, so he can't move his feet a centimeter, and THEN start tickling his soles. The more restricted someone's motion is, typically, the more ticklish. Making a person's feet immobile, and then tickling the sole produces extreme sensations which are sure to make for an interesting session.

Figure 11 – Man in Stockade

In my early career as a tickler, I didn't own stocks, but I had a reasonable facsimile; I had a futon, who's arm railings were slatted and just large enough to fit a foot through. After the submissive inserted their foot, I'd take an ankle restraint and affix it to the foot, making it too wide to withdraw from the slates. Instant foot restraint without the stockade! I used that set up for many years (you can see it in use in the video "Lights Out" that I made with Bondagejeopardy.com).

Alternatives to Bed Bondage and Other Thoughts

Another consideration with bondage concerns standing verses lying down. Beds are convenient for tying, but next time you are in a location with inner French doors, try this trick. Obtain 4 standard dog collars. These can be hooked around the hinges of a set of French doors. Open the doors, and you can see the hinges. You will keep the doors open during the scene. Once the dog collars are hooked in place, you can close the doors until you are ready to use them for bondage. The dog collars are virtually undetectable with the doors are shut. When ready, open the doors, then hook your Submissives restraints to the "D" rings of the dog collars; ankles and wrists. The benefits are you can reach 95% of your sub's body from this position, and fucking him standing can really blow his mind. Tickling him from this position will keep him reeling, as you can reach back and front alike. Only downside…you can't reach their soles. If the TOPS of their feet are ticklish though, you will have put them in a position where they cannot move an inch, and are helpless to your tickling. Additionally, if your desire is to tickle your submissive into wetting himself, tying him standing adds gravity to the mix. This will increase the pressure on the bladder, and make holding out much harder for your submissive.

NOTE: *In the few scenes where a submissive of mine was made to lose his bladder, he was standing (and we were outside!) Those with water sports tendencies can acquire a small child's inflatable pool in which your submissive will stand, if you wish to tickle the piss out of them indoors! And be aware that when a person loses control of their bladder while being tickled...they LOSE CONTROL. This means they will pee without the ability to stop it. That could be quite a long time, and is totally related to the level of hysteria you have induced.*

If outside, tying your submissive between two trees can also be highly effective. Make sure the trees are about 6 feet apart (far enough distance so your submissive can stand and spread their arms and not hit either tree.) Having said this let me add a few comments. It's easy to romanticize the allure of sex in the wilderness. We read stories all the time of the errant fuck in the woods. But the reality of the situation is unless it's winter, bugs are a factor.

89

Either slather your bodies in some bug repellent beforehand, or resign yourself to mosquito, chigger, spider or tick bites. Also, no one likes snakes, but in the wild trappings of a wooded area, snakes can be a consideration. If you are extremely remote, wild animals pose additional considerations. The last thing you want is your favorite submissive, naked, tied between two trees, smelling of sex when that mountain lion or grizzly bear appears. **Bring a good sharp knife with you.** It will serve for defense as well as provide an easy way to cut ropes. If you have taken my earlier advice and used restraints that buckle to your SUB's wrists and ankles, then you can simply cut the tether ropes to them, and your SUB is free. Also make sure you aren't on land that's owned by someone else. One of the most embarrassing moments of my life entailed tying a lover to some trees in a heavily wooded area in rural Oklahoma. We were home visiting his grandparents, and had decided to go "hiking". In an area that was sparsely populated, we had no idea the land on which we hiked was owned by the local flake, and he regularly walked his property to dissuade trespassers. There was my Sub tied naked between two trees, and I look up to see, about 100 yards away, some old coot yelling at us "perverts". There was just enough time to cut him loose, gather our clothes and make a run for the truck. Visions of Deliverance abound, but in rural Oklahoma, the last thing we wanted was a confrontation with a local shotgun while trespassing. Be careful. Be sane. A little forethought will make this go much easier.

Have nowhere to tie your submissive's hands? I purchased something called "portable dungeon" straps to help with this problem. These are comprised of two wide leather strips about a foot long, that each have 1" length of small PVC tube sewn into their ends, and "D" rings sewn to their other end. You simply open a door, flip the PVC side over the top of the door (leaving the "D" ring side on your side of the door), close and lock the door. Now you have two "D" rings which can be used for tethering your Sub's wrist restraints. When pulled, the PVC side can't clear the door top and effectively creates a secure bondage point. This is GREAT for use in hotels; I've never really had a use for those adjoining doors between rooms. But now it's not wasted space.

Figure 12 – Portal Dungeon Straps

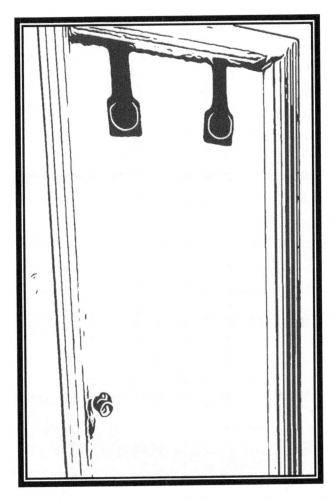

Figure 13 – Portal Dungeon Straps on Door

Another option is an EMT board. Typically, these are used by Emergency rooms and ambulances, and since they haven't normally been used by fetishists, they are damn cheap and fit easily under a bed or in a closet. On eBay, you can grab one for under $50 and they are perfect for tying someone, as they have multiple holes along an inflexible hard plastic board.

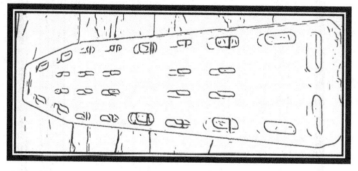

Figure 14 – EMT Board

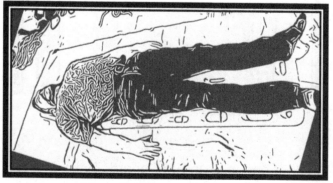

Figure 15 – Man on EMT Board

Other conventional Bondage devices can also be used like a Lucifer chair, spanking or fuck benches, St. Andrew crosses, and even a cage. Rather than describe each device, I'll leave you to a few searches on the Internet.

Blindfolding Your Submissive and Deprivation

Blindfolding a submissive can effectively notch up the intensity of the play to proportions that many will find uncomfortable if not undesirable. Much of tickling is related to surprise and the mental state of the submissive. Many men steel themselves against a tickling attack and the ability to see where or when it's coming is enough to allow them to fight losing control. Take away their sight, and they quickly become helpless, unable to deal with tickling when they don't know from whence it comes!

Often men will "challenge" me with being able to fend it off. I like to ask submissives if they were ticklish as kids, and to what degree. If someone was ticklish as a kid, you can bet good money they can be broken (successfully tickled). Blinding is an integral part of this. Sleeping masks provide a decent blindfold, as do standard blindfolds from leather supply stores. However, I have found that most designs are fairly ineffective for really blocking out all sight. Light always creeps in around the nose. And where there's light, there's sight.

To fix this problem is simple. Take a tissue and fold it into a small square. Then place this over the eye BETWEEN the eye and the blindfold. Do this with both eyes and anything you choose to use as a blindfold will work: bandannas, sleeping masks, leather blindfolds. The Submissive literally MUST close their eyes, when tissue is put over their eye socket.

Since sensory deprivation is the key to the efficacy of using blindfolds, it only follows that taking away additional senses might very well enhance a tickling session. Hoods block both sight and sound, and come in a variety of types, styles and textures. Leather hoods that lace up are normally fun, as they normally have grommets and "D" rings affixed to them, adding additionally bondage configuration possibilities. Imagine your Sub, in fist mitts, hands bound behind him, in a leather hood. He can't see. He can't really hear, and he is completely vulnerable. When you start tickling, that's all he is going to focus on. There are no other distractions, and the feeling of helplessness and of being trapped will only escalate your Submissive's ticklishness. My favorite hood is a Lycra hood with a sewn in blindfold. Why? Well I can touch my submissive's face during the scene and the Lycra will increase that sensation. Want to send a Sub through the roof? Put a Lycra hood on him and then run a finger along his upper lip. Combine that with some tickling to the torso and your submissive is going to laugh his ass off.

Mummification

If you have a submissive that has excruciatingly ticklish feet you might want to consider mummification as a bondage method. This is a method of wrapping your Sub from head to toe with normally his feet, dick, and mouth open, and everything else encased in duct tape. I know you are thinking "ouch" for when this is removed, but actually the process entails encasing their body in plastic wrap first, and then following it with duct tape.

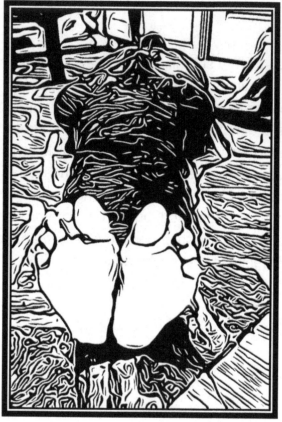

Figure 16 – Mummified with Feet Exposed

NOTE: This is extremely hot and your submissive will sweat profusely while in this kind of bondage. Care should be taken to supervise your submissive at all times while they are in this kind of bondage and should NEVER be left alone even for a few moments. Cramping or inability to breath can take this scene from excellent to disastrous in a blink of an eye. With the intensity of this kind of bondage comes the need for more care.

Figure 17 – Mummified with Gag

Although the task seems daunting, the actual effort to mummify someone isn't that hard. To mummify someone, have them strip down, place a towel under their left arm, between their left arm and their body, running lengthwise armpit to hip. Do the same with the right arm.   And place a towel lengthwise between the legs. This will prevent the bones of the elbow and knees from rubbing and irritating the skin, as well as provide something to absorb sweat that your Submissive is going to generate in a huge way. Then begin wrapping in sections. First wrap the ankles to the knees. Encase both legs as a single unit. Wrap the Cling wrap a few times, and then using a role of duct tape, wrap the tape repeatedly over the plastic wrap until the complete length from ankle to knee is bound. Be sure to keep the

Figure 18 – Mummified for Tickling

soles of the feet exposed and uncovered. Then wrap more cling wrap, this time from the shoulders to the waist. Have your Sub inflate his lungs to their fullest, so the wrap doesn't compress his lungs. This is a typical mistake of first-time wrappers. Tickling is going to require your submissive to breath, and once completely bound, if their lungs are compressed, they could suffocate. Especially since the skin is completely encased and will be unable to breath in any way.   Wrap the whole upper torso as a single unit; pinning the arms to the body. Make sure you're encircle them three or more times, and then follow with the duct tape again. Then repeat the process from bellybutton to below the knee. It's important the two regions you just wrapped overlap. However, when around the cock, after wrapping with cling wrap, punch a hole in the cling wrap and pull the cock AND balls through the opening. Then duct tape carefully around that region being sure to leave the balls and dick flying free in the air.   Lastly repeat the process with the head, affixing it to the shoulders, and leaving a hole for only the mouth.   Once this is done, then tickle your submissive's feet to your hearts content! You will find them wickedly confined, and unable to move, which heightens the sensations.

> Pro tip - I'll often put my submissive into fist mitts
> first, and then mummify them. That way they can't use
> their fingers to try and poke through siren and tape.

While creating the artwork for this section, a friend of mine shared another trick to short cut the process. Instead of cling wrap, use garbage bags. Have your submissive stand in one garbage bag, towel between his legs, and use duct tape to tape the legs together up to the hands. Then put another garbage bag over their head (poking a hole through it to make a kind of plastic poncho) and then tape from shoulders down. Tear small holes at the feet, and duct tape around the ankles to secure the whole. This made the mummification process much quicker, and was equally as effective.

Where to Find Bondage Gear

Lastly a comment about where you can procure the items I have mentioned in this section. First and foremost, try … EBAY (www.ebay.com)! Yes, people across the world purchase bondage gear and then for one reason or another realize it's not what they want, or they come up with an extra, upgrade to better, marry a nun, etc. Leather Masks run $150 or more in specialty shops. On EBAY, you can sometimes get one for $75 that's brand new, once the bidding is over.

Also check out the vendor stands at various Leather man gatherings mentioned in the "Where to Meet The Tickle Tribe" section. Most of the leather events boast a huge bazaar area in which everything from bondage videos to bondage racks can be purchased.   I highly suggest waiting on making those purchases until the last day of the event though; venders are often eager to ditch stuff they brought to sell (versus having to lug them home), and are willing to make extremely good deals!

There are many vendors out there that make and sell great equipment. Mr. S. Leather and Fort Troff are two of my favorite places to go to get bondage gear. Use Google to find them online.

The Erotic Theater

---

*The man slowly approached
the building. He tried the door
handle and it easily gave to his
touch. The owner had
forgotten to lock the door.
Quietly he slipped inside and
began searching the darkened
house. Room by room he
searched until he entered the
master bedroom. The Robber
swung his flashlight in a wide
arc, and as hc turned away
from a closet that was partially
open, he felt a force knock him
forward onto the bed. The
flashlight skittered across the
floor, knocked from his hand.
A blanket was tossed over his
head and as the robber
struggled to remove it, a
handcuff locked closed around
his wrist. Its other end was
already locked to the
headboard of the wrought iron*

bed frame. The robber struggled more, but was easily subdued as a second pair of handcuffs locked his only free hand above his head. He was still covered with the blanket when he felt his shirt yanked from his pants, and hands slide underneath…like a python ready to strike its prey, the owner's hands slithered their way to the soft ticklish spots on the robbers torso; both tensed as the tickling began. "THINK YOU'RE GONNA ROB ME, DO YOU!" the owner growled as he tickled with abandon. Suddenly, the robber felt his belt buckle snapped open and pulled free of his pants. "What the fuck are you ….hahahahahahahahahaha" the robber's complaint was lost amidst the laughter he was forced to expel…as the owner dug into his ribs, wiggling his thumbs in order to bring the man to hysteria.

Disoriented by the tickle, the robber could barely speak as the owner roughly yanked his pants and underwear down…

A story from an internet website? No…it's a step by step accounting of a role-play session that I once had. The sub was told to arrive at a specific time, to bring a flashlight, and to search the house for a bottle of lube that would be left on a counter. I left no lube out, and hid in the closet, waiting for him to arrive, handcuffs already attached to the headboard (hidden under pillows) and had a blanket in hand to blind him. Did the SUB know how it was going to play out? No. And during the whole night, he was the robber, and I was the owner who had caught him in the act and was now going to make him pay. The tickling that night was fierce, and the guy was hard from the moment he was handcuffed until he was brought to climax three hours later.

In previous chapters I discussed how important setting the scene was. The example used was a SUB/DOM scene – which lends itself to power exchange. Most tickle role-playing scenes revolve around the "unwilling victim" who has something great to lose if they don't cooperate. The robber was going to be turned over to the police if he didn't do as told. The fact that I overpowered him and restrained him beforehand simply established the authority. The whole session was predicated on the fact we both played our roles and knew them. As the DOM, I gave my Sub enough information to play his role, but didn't let him know how it would really play out. Afterward, my submissive confessed to me it was the best role-play he had ever done. When I pressed him for why, his only response was "it felt real".

Role-playing is synonymous with play-acting. Pretend. And the more props and setting you add to the session, the better it will be for all players. Keep the roles up. Keep it "on-stage" until such a time as the scene has ended, or the safe-word has been used. A simple lapse of calling a partner his actual name (when your character would never have known the name of this "intruder') is enough to break the spell we call "suspension of disbelief". It's like watching a play and then having one of the stage actors forget a line and say, "Damn…what's that line!" Role-playing has the same dynamic. We buy into the moment. We pretend we are there and say things those characters in that situation would say. And if all parties engaged are playing at the same reality, explosive sexual conclusions are inevitable.

I can already hear your question – when did the negotiation for the scene occur? It occurred at the same time you are negotiating the role-play. The Dom and Sub still have to agree what the parameters of the scene are, and the Dom, regardless of the acting, has to conform to these rules and honor safewords. Typically, there is a text exchange, email exchange and/or phone call in which everything is established BEFORE the meeting occurs. I like to go to lunch with the sub and talk, but any method you prefer works, as long as its discussed. Once the role-play has started is NOT the time to start asking about what is or isn't acceptable. Role-play scenes

have a discrete beginning and end; once it has
started, the players have to stay in the moment
to maintain the energy of the fantasy.

The following is a list of some of my favorite
tickle role-playing games. This list is in no way
comprehensive, and play-acting during sex is
only limited by the imagination.

The Coach

The setting of this scene is a locker room, or simply a weight bench. It might begin in an office. The Coach has a clip board with a roster. A whistle is easy to acquire and goes a long way to help create the role of the athletic authority figure. The teammate, in clothing appropriate to the sport of choice (wrestling is my favorite), has reported to the coach's office. Unfortunately, the teammate has done something that now requires the coach to remove him from the team. The team member pleads…he "NEEDS" to be on the team…he'll be humiliated if he gets taken off the roster…he'll do "anything" to stay. The coach should respond to the word "anything" and explain that he needs help… How or where the DOM takes the coach role should be tailored to the likes and desires of both players.   I often explain I had discovered the teammate was too ticklish. A liability for the wrestling team, as the teammate could easily be eliminated if tickled during a wrestling match. Tickle training is required to stay on the team. He begrudgingly agrees to being tied down for aversion therapy for tickling. The coach ties down the boy, insisting on him being in his underwear (to prevent cutting off blood circulation), and the scene progresses from there. The coach explores every inch of the teammates body repeatedly…searching to the most ticklish places so the teammate can learn to control his laughter. Of course, he cannot…and this makes the scene all that more interesting. The Coach should INSIST the teammate try and fight the sensations, trying not to laugh.

Frat House Hazing

There isn't a gay porn magazine on the rack that doesn't include at least one story of college fraternity hazing taken to the limit. This scene has the pledge master forcing his frat plebes into doing whatever he requires, if they want to be let into the fraternity. It's Rush week, and every pledge wants in.

Often College Frats force their pledges to memorize long paragraphs of nonsense, and then they are required to regurgitate them on command. Provide the paragraph to your SUBMISSIVE via email the day before they arrive. Make it something fairly complicated, but something you will know is wrong if he makes a mistake. Instruct your "pledge" that the following paragraph should be learned by heart.   The Preamble of the United States Constitution is wicked in this context, but something you can easily make a case of his having to know.

> "**We the people of the United States, in order to form a more**

perfect union, establish justice, insure domestic tranquility, provide for the common defense, promote the general welfare, and secure the blessings of liberty to ourselves and our posterity, do ordain and establish this constitution for the United States of America."

Once again, the setting can easily be a house, the clothing simple college shirts, and the props...well anything that lends itself to tickling. Both partners need to establish the college vernacular, and this scene lends itself to a good hogtie. This is accomplished by having the Pledge lay on his stomach, hands should be tied together, and ankles tied together, and then the two should be tied with a separate rope to each other, behind the back of the subject.

When working with rope, be sure to use knots that don't tighten with pulling (there are many books on rope bondage, I suggest Jay

Wisemans ***Erotic Bondage handbook***) A trick of mine is to wrap their ankles and wrists with heavy athletic socks before tying rope around the limbs. If you really want to blow their mind, also put a sock OVER their whole hand, creating a make shift fist mitt. It pretty well makes the fingers useless; eliminating any possibility your quarry will untie themselves.

Once the pledge is hogtied, then his shoes can be removed and feet tickled, or he can be rolled on his back, shirt lifted and torso tickled (as well as dick played with). I suggest this twist to the scene – once the submissive is tied; tickle him while having him say the paragraph. If he can't say it, because he is too ticklish, then you continue tickling until he DOES say it. If he DOES say it, then you make him say it again…and again. If he gets a word wrong…that earns him another 15 minutes of tickling. If he says any words besides the paragraph penalize him with more time required. Make it a helpless situation, one in which he can't possibly win, and then make him endure the tickling as punishment. The pledge will endure it all, because he wants to be in the fraternity.

The Spy

Ah, the spy who knew too much. Or too little. The scene is interrogation. The spy has been captured, and you are going to tickle the information out of him. As with the robber scene, the top should surprise the spy, catching him in the act of rifling state secrets, and get him restrained. The Spy knows some form of torture is going to be used upon him, but has no clue that tickling would be used to exact information from him.

The DOM, after securing the SPY should make a big deal of removing his shoes, oiling up the soles of his feet, and talking about how horrible it's going to be if the spy doesn't "tell all he knows". DEMAND to know what he has stolen. What secrets has he leaked? To whom did he share the stolen information? How did he do it? Your sub will be reeling as he tries to formulate answers to these questions that really don't have a good answer. Best to keep him blindfolded and to use lots of bondage positions in this scene. And keep up the tickling until you break him. You'll know the moment – it's when he can no longer form sentences, and is giggling hysterically without the ability to resist. He won't be pulling on his restraints anymore; he won't have the strength.

A buddy of mine once bragged he had played this scene with his submissive, but had never tickled the submissive in the 5 years they had been together. He never mentioned tickling, and had been waiting for the right moment to use it in their play.   His experience with the Sub indicated he wasn't just ticklish…he was hyper ticklish. The Submissive, who got off on pain, loved the idea of being tortured for information until the Dom started oiling his bare soles. The DOM explained that he wanted to leave no marks, and therefore a different method of "persuasion" would be used. Expecting Bastinado, the Submissive was totally caught off guard and dissolved into a mass of uncontrollable laughter that escalated to extreme proportions within a matter of minutes.   Supposedly the scene turned into a water sports scene as the Submissive shamefully wet himself, unprepared for the intense tickling.

Peasant and the King

If you are a DOM and own a set of stocks,
don't let this game go unplayed...especially if
you have a sub with ticklish feet. In early days
of Camelot ala renaissance faire, the town thief
or anyone who was being punished would be
locked into stocks. Their hands were
restrained (either in an upper set of stocks, or
tied behind their backs), and then they were
subjected to whatever punishment the
townspeople thought appropriate. This often-
included tickling. Stories abound of men in the
stockade whose feet were covered in brine,
and goats were led to them to lick and torment
them.   The goats, unattended, would lick the
soles of the restrained men for hours. In this
scene, after locking your submissive into the
stocks, try and exact some information from
him. DEMAND he tell you where the stolen
item was, or with whom he has in cahoots.
Your sub won't be able to answer these
questions. He will beg and plead for you to
stop the tickling, but you proceed until he
either admits what you are accusing him of...in

which case you REALLY tickle him to excess… or until he can't laugh any more.

Once, a SUB of mine and I were visiting the house of a DOM we knew in San Francisco. He had a fully outfitted dungeon, and we had been simply checking out the space around 6 PM. The room was multi-leveled, and a four-poster bed with wheel and pulleys adorned the upper tier. Below was a sling, an Andrew's cross, a collection of various whips and restraints, and a puppy cage pushed to the corner. The full stocks were in another corner of a lower level and my SUB continued to monkey around with the setup. Finally, I ordered him to strip to his jockstrap and placed him into the stocks, after telling him three times to "leave that equipment alone". He thought it was all a joke, and that we'd play and then get ready for the party. I asked if he could pull his feet free, and he was unable to. Then I cuffed his hands behind his back and tied them to the bench on which he sat. A play party was to start around 8 pm. And having been pissed off by his constant attention to the space and not to me, (and also assuming the area had been cleaned and set up for the party that was to ensue) I figured to teach him a lesson. I went upstairs, leaving him restrained; his feet sticking out of secure stocks, hands cuffed behind him. My host and I talked about the play party and he agreed to allow me to punish my Sub during it. At 7:45 I went back to the dungeon and hooded him. Then I wrote with a black indelible magic marker "TICKLE ME" across the soles of his feet. Along his back I wrote TICKLE MY RIBS. Of course, he had no idea what I had written, and the hood prevented him from having a clue about what was about to happen.   When party members started to arrive, they were a little puzzled by my Sub, but soon found out how ticklish he was when they started following my written orders. Three men stayed glued to that stockade all night. The Sub howled and pleaded, but all were told he was being punished and disregarded anything he said. And I've got to tell you ...that Sub never disobeyed me again. As a side note, it also jump started the play party – which is often an issue with sex parties. Someone has to start, then everyone gets into the game.

Slave Instructions

I love a good surprise, and so do most
Submissives. This role-play entails providing
an envelope at the door which the SUB is to
read when he arrives. I remember one sub that
was instructed to hood himself (complete with
a lace up back), to gag himself (the gag had a
hole in the center of it so there was zero
obstruction to the airway), to restrain his
ankles, and then to handcuff himself to a chair.
The position in which he locked himself made
mobility impossible. His instructions indicated
he was to leave his clothing in the large paper
grocery bag that had been left with all the
bondage gear inside. And he was given a time
limit in which to restrain himself. I, of course,
was hiding within the house and waited and
listened as the submissive came in, stripped,
and locked himself in. Once he was helpless
and blind, I came in, making a lot of noise as I
removed the brown bag. Then I tickled and
tormented him…saying nothing. No words
were spoken the whole session. If you give
your sub no way to communicate, be sure you

monitor him constantly. Don't leave the room for 10 minutes, because should anything block his airway, you would want to be there for assistance. When we were done, I removed his handcuffs and left the house. He had been instructed that once the handcuffs were removed to wait 5 minutes, remove his bondage, and then leave the house. I hid before his hood came off, and he never knew for sure if I was the one that had used him or not. This scene makes Submissives wild! There is something sexually charged about the idea of having no clue with whom you just had sex. Every person that Sub sees in a bar from that day forward could be the person who used him during the Slave instruction game. And what DOM hasn't introduced some of his leather friends to his submissive once the submissive is hooded? Many! Because most understand that creating sexual mystery for a Submissive is a powerful reward, and keeps the submissive engaged in the scene long after it has physically ended.

The Robber

The setting as earlier described in the opening is the location being burgled. The Sub should wear dark clothing, and maybe a mask or hood. Surprise is important in this play, and the DOM should devise a way to turn the tables on the robber so as to gain the authority stance in the scene. A plastic gun is enough to threaten a robber with violence to get him restrained (if wrestling your robber is undesirable) …this can be fun as the robber is forced to perhaps strip…or maybe handcuff himself…while the DOM threatens him with being shot.   In my scene, I preferred the wrestling to get him locked into handcuffs, but however it's done, the owner is looking for revenge and the robber will pay the price of having invaded the owner's home. Another take on this is a role reversal. The DOM is the robber, and catches the owner under gunpoint…ties him up as part of the robbery, only to find the owner insanely ticklish. The robber then proceeds to tickle the owner into telling him where the valuables in the house are stored. Either variation plays well, as the setting is a house. It's typical in this situation to have the "home owner" hide something which the robber must persuade them to disclose...for example car keys... "where are the car keys". And the tickling continues until the location is revealed!

The Job Seeker

The setting of this scene is an office or a warehouse. The interviewer has a job application made up, and the beginning of the scene should include forcing the applicant to fill out a mock job application. Both parties begin outfitted in dress clothing appropriate for an office job. This can easily be modified to a construction site though, where combat boots and torn jeans might be apropos. Once again, it should be tailored to the desires and interests of the players. The applicant really needs a job and would do "Anything" to get it. Once again, the Dom should cue on the offer of "anything". I've played this scene with a slightly different twist once, quite successfully; the applicant was asked to help me test out some bondage equipment that the "company" sold. Once restrained, I commented on his hard on, which began the tickling component of the scene. I started to undress him, and he had no choice but to cooperate, or risk not getting the job. If the job Seeker complains about his clothing being removed, the interviewer should threaten the loss of opportunity. The scene progresses until the interviewer has all he wants. Once done, the applicant is told if he wants the job, not only should he keep secrecy, but he should also report to help test out ALL the other bondage equipment, every Friday night after the warehouse closes.

How to Throw a Tickle Party

Because the tickling community is fairly fragmented, it's often hard to find people to tickle or who would like to be tickled. Over the years, as I've met various tickle enthusiasts, I've started throwing tickle parties – gatherings for men to meet others who share the interest of tickling. And invariably, these kinds of parties can be less than desirable, as people awkwardly stand around, waiting for someone to make the first move.

Given this issue, I devised a way to guarantee everyone at a tickle party has fun.

You will need a bag of multi-color poker chips. In a bag place two chips of each color. Keep the party invites to 2 times the number of bondage "stations" you have set up for players.

➢ Everyone strips to their underwear at the door as they enter.

➢ Everyone picks a random chip from a bag.

➤ Throughout my house are bondage
   stations, each associated with a color
   which matches the chips.
   a. Sling
   b. Stocks
   c. Bondage bed
   d. Spanking bench
   e. Lucifer chair
   f. An Inversion table

➤ Each person finds the other person who
   got the matching color chip, and then
   goes to the bondage area associated
   with the color they picked.

➤ The two people negotiate who will tickle
   and who will be the ticklee. If both are
   ticklees they can trade with other
   couples who might be ticklers (or
   switches), but in general, this pairing
   system works best. Typically, most
   people into tickling enjoy both being
   tickled and tickling. In over 50 parties, it
   has never been an issue with any
   attendees.

➤ Provide name tags, and have people
   write "TICKLER", "TICKLEE", or

"SWITCH" to self-identify their play preference along with their name.

➢ If an odd number of people show up, I will act as the dungeon master for the evening; I will walk around and make sure people are respecting limits and assist in whatever way is needed to ensure fun is had by all. In general, I try to do this regardless, but the point is sometimes it's an odd number.

➢ Throughout the house I post party rules for play, and everyone is expected to follow them (see the next section for my Tickle party rules).

Using this format ensures everyone who attends, plays. And after the first scene, people who may want to hook up can run another scene. Once the first sessions are done, the rest of the party is handled in a free format, when a piece of equipment becomes available, first one to grab it, gets it. After the first scene you can play with whoever agrees to play.

Everyone appreciates being able to participate, and because I make sure I only invite people I know, people are friendly, and the gathering is predictable.

Primarily, the most important thing is to take initiative and set expectations! If you are hosting the party, think about how you want it to succeed. Is there going to be food? Towels? Where will people sit? Will you provide equipment for people? Do they need to bring their own lube? Where will people go to get away from the action if they need a break? Etc. Write up the most important things and post them for people. When everyone arrives, take a minute and ask if all understand the party rules. Don't worry that people will be offended – it's your party.

ERIK11's Tickle Party Rules

TICKLE PARTY RULES

This is a consensual, safe place. Discretion is agreed and required due to the fetish nature of the gathering.

Everyone coming is into Edging, Bondage and Tickling.

1. What ERIK11 say's, goes. Period. He is the dungeon master

2. Don't like it? Refer to rule number one.

3. It's your job to clean up the play space, toys, rewrap rope, etc. after you use it. Paper and regular towels as well as cleaning solution will be provided.

4. NO INTERCOURSE. Not that kind of party. This is about tickling, and edge play while being bound.

5. All Nudity / Bondage / etc. is negotiated before a scene. Once a scene starts, no one can join in that

hasn't already been given permission during the initial negotiation to join. You can jack someone off if the ticklee agrees to it during the negotiation.

6. All scenes will include a safeword for the ticklee to use

7. Once a scene has started, another can be brought into an existing scene if and only if the top and bottom ask them. This cannot be solicited once the scene has started.

These are the rules I have for my tickle gatherings. I post them publicly, and everyone knows them before anyone plays. Your parties may have differing rules. The point is you take the time to communicate them to level set — when you leave the structure of a gathering to spontaneity, often undesirable events can occur.

What Does SIR Want?

Brad had gone for days
without masturbating. Jon had
told him he had to wait for at
least a week without climax
before they could play again
and now it seemed like he was
going mad with the desire to
blow his load. Twice during the
night, he had woken up with a
drooling tent pole marking his
sheets, as his sleeping body
emphasized his need for
release. It had been years
since he had gone this long
denying himself and he was
going mad. Jon often made
requests of him; what clothing
to wear; what things to say,
questions about his fantasies
and likes and dislikes; direct,
simple protocols to follow. He
never knew what to expect
and he never tried guessing.
The sessions had gone from

simple to complex, and the fact Brad now had a playmate who shared his interest in role-playing and kink blew his mind completely. In the past, he had tried to get boyfriends to be more aggressive. But ultimately it was impossible to get that vanilla date to the point of taking complete control. There was always a void with them. He liked someone else to take the lead and his personal fantasies revolved around pleasing another man; whatever he required. Brad had taken many years to get a hold of his complete sexual identity. He didn't question his desires, he merely knew what they were, and he had enough life experience to know it was best when played out this way. Nothing from his Top's body was considered dirty. He would lick, suck, touch or try anything that would sexually excite his partner. And Jon knew exactly how to press his buttons. Just like now, sitting on his bed, reeling from the unbridled waves of erotic need, he couldn't stop thinking about the scene that would soon occur. He hoped he would please Jon and be able to comply with all his demands and keep him interested enough to continue playing. Ten days ago, Jon had left a bag at the front door with instructions and various leather gear for him to put on before entering the house. That scene had been a wild ride for sure. And just when he thought there wasn't something they had already done; Jon would pop another surprise on him and raise the stakes of the game a little more. Forcing him not to climax was new. And although he remembered telling Jon chastity play interested him, he had perceived little, if any, interest in it from Jon at the

time. Now, he flipped on his
stomach and dry humped his
bed sheets. Certain only that
he must not allow things to get
out of hand, but hardly able to
contain himself. Jon was
driving him wild, even though
he was all the way across
town!

Up until this point, the assumption has been
this book is being read by someone fairly
experienced with SUB/DOM play. But if you
are a curious reader, with no knowledge of
this kind of interaction, your thoughts may be
of puzzlement. Why would a person subject
themselves to the whims of another,
especially if it involves elements of the
unknown, elements of extreme energy swings
and/or power exchange? Why would
someone allow themselves to be tied down,
or to be tickle tortured? How could this
possibly be construed as sexual activity?

It's far easier to understand if you consider
this as a partnership of desires. Akin to "It's

only rape if you don't want it." Without analyzing the sexual psyches of every type of ego and id in the world, and without addressing the childhood traumas or experiences that potentially make a person sexually desire what they do, it's simply a case of "boys will be boys." There is no need to be concerned with the why. If the activity is safe, is desired by both parties, and agreed upon beforehand, then why not?

Brad's thoughts in the story capture the exact thoughts of many submissives; "I will do what it takes to please my partner."

Submissives find the thought of being challenged by their dominator sexually exciting. The more ardent the challenge, the more satisfying their sexual release becomes. I've met many submissives who neither required nor desired climax as part of their sexual play. Often, they are ordered not to cum. Period. This titillates them, and makes it even more exciting. Now they must completely own the responsibility of pleasing the DOM without consideration to themselves in any form. What higher form of allegiance could they display? Not only are they trusting with abandon (barring the boundaries set between the two players), they are also giving of themselves to whatever need the DOM has (sometimes for weeks at a time).

Once a submissive friend of mine explained he considered himself the "top" in his relationship. Not because he was the one fucking, but because he was the one responsible for his partner's climax. He was the one that made his partner cum, either anally or orally, and therefore, he was the real person with the power – not his dominant partner. His comment was "without me, he's left to masturbation." It certainly changed my perspective of a submissive's viewpoint.

And never forget the bravest man in the room is the submissive!

And the DOM? What of him? Once again, why ask why? There are many reasons people desire command of another. The point is, for a DOM, it gets them sexually excited.

It's what "floats their boat." And as a DOM, there are many responsibilities to the scene which fall into their court. I've already addressed many of them – preparation, setting the mood, leading the scene, establishing trust, determining (and observing) boundaries, establishing authority and maintaining surprise.   Successful Dom's have a tone to their voice when dealing with submissives. It's a tone of certainty. Of knowing the intended outcome, and having no doubt the "goal" will be achieved. It doesn't have to be framed in anger, but it does have to leave no room for question. Be specific with orders provided to a submissive. And provide corrections to your submissive when they forget or don't follow your request (especially if you have specifically indicated a consequence for not complying). Getting corrected is as exciting a component to the scene for the submissive as the correcting is to the Dom.   Often a submissive will act out in order to _receive_ the punishment, because they know the form the punishment will take will be sexually exciting for the Dom to administer.

With this knowledge, it should become obvious the game is to play this dynamic to the hilt. Give your Submissive orders which are hard to accomplish, or which they will surely fail. Setup rules and wait for the submissive to cross the line you've defined. Given 40 rules, they're going to slip eventually. And the more tired your playmate becomes, the more prone they are to err. If your submissive shows up 10 minutes late, punish him for wasting your time, which can never be returned. You can bet the submissive was planning on getting the punishment, if you've told them to be there at a specific time and they are late. And how should you punish them? Well tickling, of course. Threaten an amount of time you will tickle them uninterrupted. Go for the spot which simply drives them mad and keep them reeling until they have done their penance.

The following is a list of actions I like to demand of my Subs when dominating. This by no means is a comprehensive list, and as with other suggestions, these are only limited by the imagination.

- **"NOSE TO THE FLOOR"** – This is a command I bark at my submissives when I want to park them for a period of time. It could be the beginning, middle, or end of the scene, but it's fairly specific and definitely puts your Sub in an extremely vulnerable position. He should drop to all fours and actually place his nose on the ground. If the Sub is about to be spanked, this is a perfect position for that expectation. I also use it as the starting point before placing them in bondage.

- **SHOES OUTSIDE** – It's amazing sometimes what simple things will yield. This is one of those "big bang for the buck" items. Have your submissive remove his shoes before entering your house. Submissives love being nude or some form of undress during a scene. Especially if the DOM stays completely clothed.   Before any Submissive is allowed to cross the threshold of my doorway, they are required to remove their shoes. Whether the socks are removed or not is totally up to the DOM and his intentions. A few times, I have had subs with particularly ticklish feet remove their shoes AND socks at the door. Then once tied, I complain that their feet are dirty, and use a scrub brush and soapy water to clean them. Talk about sending a guy into uncontrolled hysterics!!!!

- **NUDE ALWAYS** – I use this for Internet chatting with Submissives, when establishing a bond. I require them to be naked when chatting with me. It's especially effective if they have a web cam and you can verify if they are indeed naked. If you have a submissive and intend on using him with others during a play party, having him completely nude when the guests arrive is also appealing. It builds the feeling of vulnerability within the submissive, and provides a slightly embarrassing moment for the Sub. After all, people will be dressed when they arrive. Have him serve drinks so his nudity is absolutely acknowledged by all at the gathering.   Write messages across his body like "Ticklish here" or "My tummy is incredibly ticklish" in indelible ink. And watch your friends have a ball with him.

- **SIR WHEN ADDRESSED BOY** – My personal preference for being addressed by a Sub is "SIR". Some people prefer "Master" others "M'lord" and even others "Daddy". Whatever your desire, you should place a protocol around the use of the title. My Subs know that if the word "BOY" is part of a statement to them, they must respond with "SIR" in the reply. If it's missed, there's an excuse for correcting them. This is particularly effective with single word answers. "Boy, have you had enough?" will almost always get back a "YES!" At which point I remind them I had addressed them with "Boy" and now they are going to have to endure another 15 minutes of tickling as punishment for breaking the protocol.

- **CLOTHING SPECIFICATIONS** – One of the perks being the DOM, is you do get to have it your way – however that may be. If you like Speedos, tell your Submissive to wear them. Into tighty-whities? Make it a requirement for play. Answers like "I don't have any" should be responded to with a simple "well I guess you will soon, huh!" Tell the submissive to wear what you enjoy. Have a thing for jock straps? Tell him the style, color, brand and whether he should wash it. If he balks, you can correct him, or tell him the scene won't happen if he doesn't wear your "uniform." Believe me, the SUB will love the task of buying clothing to wear for you. Remember, ultimately, he wants to please you. Of course, requesting a college kid to wear a diamond tiara will just lose you subs, so keep the requests sane and you will get your preference. If you've played with your Sub and he's done particularly well, then you might buy him a piece of clothing you'd like to see him in as a reward, and then force him to wear it as part of the scene. Then, when he leaves, he has a souvenir of the encounter. Odds are, he'll sleep with it and dream of you.

- **CLEAN INSIDE AND OUT** – Although some people have a penchant for toilet play, I personally find excrement distasteful during sex. I don't want to see it, smell it, or experience it in any form. My Subs are told to be clean inside and out, and "anything that comes out of your butt may end up in your mouth, so be sure to take your time." Let's face it. If it's about the DOM's likes, then you have to be very specific about these kinds of things. Want him to shave his pubes? Shave his ass? Tell him. (Personally, I prefer a Sub with close trimmed pubes, that way I can put cock rings on him without having to worry about pulling hair, and smooth skin is far more sensitive than skin covered with hair.) And obviously, the opposite also applies. Like a guy to be ripe? Tell your Submissive not to wash for a few days. He may whine about it, but you can bet he's going to love you for your stern attitude, your command of the scene, and your keen awareness of what you like in a man. When finishing a scene, I often will cum on my Sub's chest and then require him to wear it on his body underneath his shirt, marking my territory when he leaves.

- **WASH THE TOYS** – Along the same vein of the previous item, I never wash toys that have been used with a Sub. They wash them. I keep a spray bottle of watered-down bleach, wet naps, towels, soap and the like in the bathroom, and as part of the end of the scene, the Sub marches in the bathroom and cleans his own toys. This is non-negotiable for me and should make sense. If a Sub knows he's going to have to clean the toys, he's going to take a little more care to be clean. And often my subs each have their own toys that they bring with them for when we play...in case I want to use it.

- **THE IMPOSSIBLE TASK** – As stated earlier, the submissive enjoys being corrected, because he knows the correction is a sexual rush for the Dominant. The Dominant can make this more fun by giving the Sub an impossible task. Often, I will find the most ticklish part of a Sub's body and then use it against him. I'll tell him "I'll give you a 15-minute break from tickling, if you can be completely silent for the next 5 minutes." For the first minute I'll work on some area of his body that isn't really that ticklish.   And then, when the Sub seems to relax, I'll launch at this most ticklish spot. It's a great moment when he breaks. If he doesn't, then he's earned the time, and you have to honor that – this doesn't mean that all activity stops. That 15-minute break time is when you can feed him your cock in some creative way. Often I'll trick them and say "I"ll give you a 15 minute break from tickling your feet"…only to immediately go to their ribs.

The illusion is a sexual scene between a Submissive and a Dom will be only what the DOM wants. The reality is, regardless of what the DOM wants, it's really what both of them want, since the submissive lives to fulfill the sexual desires (be what they may) of the dominator.   As the Chapter title indicates – it revolves around "What does SIR want?" But ultimately, it's a dance of mutual desires.

The Art of the Tickle

The scene has been set. Negotiations are done. Bondage has been secured. It's time for the Dominant partner to rock the submissive's world through sensations. No big deal, right? It's easy. Just poke them in the ribs and you're a master tickler! Not so. Just like anything related to the human being there are subtleties that are part of the act of tickling. Yes. Poking someone in the ribs can make them squeal. But can you get them to opened up energetically and laughing consistently? Can you get them to the point where a feather elicits as much response as a finger poke? Can you tickle your partner without bruising them? Or take your partner from violation to acceptance of being tickled? It takes finesse.

Let's start with the one place that everyone is ticklish. Here it is folks. The moment you've been waiting for in the book where I give you the secret keys to the tickle kingdom. The

most ticklish place on a person's body is …
their brain.   That's right. Getting someone
into the headspace is critical for them to open
up to the sensation of being tickled. You get in
their head. The following are some techniques
for shortening that time it takes to get your
partner to the state of hypersensitivity.

Neuro-Linguistic Programming (NLP)

In the field of hypnosis, there is a sub category called Neuro-linguistic programming, in which people have a pseudo automatic response associating sound with actions. It's a common thing we all do as humans. For example, many of us are programmed that the sound of a police siren makes us immediately stop. The sound of a something has caused us to react. Think about the phrase "Don't think about Purple Frogs." What's the first thing you do? Think about a purple frog. It's how humans are wired. "WATCH OUT" will cause most humans to duck or immediately take cover. "FIRE" will make people jump up and run.   Why do we do this? It's a form of NLP. Human beings innately are programmed to respond to sound. Consciously and Subconsciously. You can literally *program* a submissive to respond to sound. When combined with some skillful tickling, you can cause a Sub to reduce

HIMSELF into uncontrollable giggles and not even touch him. This is the headspace one seeks to maximize a tickle session.

Humans are hard wired through most people's childhoods that the phrase "Are you ticklish" is followed by a touch which elicits ticklish sensations. Announcing the tickling is going to happen sets the expectation that something is going to tickle. Could you tickle someone without saying a word...? This totally depends on the initial sensitivity of the person. Some people take no work whatsoever to get into the headspace. Some will take a little "unlocking".   It's a highly tuned application of Neural linguistic programming. We hear something, we experience a sensation. We hear the same thing. We experience that same sensation again. We hear the same thing....no sensation stimulus... our brain sets up the expectation that we are about to experience that sensation. This basic human tendency is critical to the master tickler.

First and foremost, blindfold your submissive. This will take away one of the senses which could distract the whole process. As mentioned in the chapter "A Frame of Mind", make sure the music that's playing (if there is music) is nothing they can 'sing along to' in their head. Make sure there's not a TV in the background to which the submissive can focus their attention. We want them paying attention.

Then use SOUND to accompany the tickle. I like to use the sound "DOINK", as I lightly poke a rib. This will almost always get a laugh. Do the sound and the poke together. Pause. Do it again. Then pause. We want their mind to begin to expect it. Do another few pokes, each time saying the word "Doink" as you do. The blindfold and the randomness of the touch will definitely get your submissive a little more sensitive. Do it a few more times…then… just say "DOINK" and do nothing. Your submissive expects the response now…and will tense awaiting the poke… the longer you wait with the action the more into the headspace they are pushed. After like 10 seconds, then actually do the poke again. I normally try and be goofy and say something funny like "oops, the battery is getting low" …and then I do it again. "Doink" – no touch, just sound…. The submissive will get antsy…they know they are about to be tickled…. They heard the sound. Once a submissive is totally in headspace, they will literally start laughing and often start pleading… this is where you want them to be. You've effectively programmed them that the sound DOINK means you're being tickled.

This dynamic can be applied a number of ways. I often will make a "blah blah blah" kind of sound with my tongue on someone's ear as I tickle their sides. I'll do it a few dozen times randomly during play… then that BLAH BLAH BLAH sound is now linked to tickling.

I also use the sound "NEE" (pronounced

knee) over and over "nee nee nee nee nee", once again while I'm tickling them. Typically, I say it while licking their neck and tickling them in another area. THIS was how someone taught ME NLP. They used this sound with tickling. And then once I was in headspace – the tickling was brutal.

Another way I apply this is through something I call "THE CLAW" – once you have your submissive hypersensitive, tell them you are going to play a game called "The CLAW". They are still blindfolded. Then say "The CLAW", out loud, and wait a random amount of time. Then grab their thigh, inner leg, waist, knee area, or underarm with your hands and furiously tickle them for 5 seconds and stop. They will burst in to laughter. Immediately say it again "THE CLAW", and once again wait a random amount of time. And then grab either the same spot or choose another, tickle furiously for 5 seconds and then stop. Then repeat it again… by the third or fourth time, your submissive will start to giggle and squirm every time they hear "THE CLAW" from that point on. This is NLP at its finest.

The sound/anticipation dynamic is a powerful part of creating a tickle scene. The anticipation and getting the submissive to expect the sensation help build a foundation to keep the play varied and lends itself to true tickle domination!

Tools of the Trade

Tony waited in silence as the master left the room. His interest in tickling had grown like wildfire. It had been almost a year since his first foray into the world of tickling. A random pickup from the Bar had led to bondage and then to tickling. He HATED to be tickled, but there was no doubt the climax he had experienced, as part of the scene truly was mind blowing. And the scene hadn't ended at that point. In fact, it went on for an additional two hours, and its intensity never waned. After that, he sought out tickling with his various play partners. Some DOM's balked at his request, and others obliged, without really being interest in the energy that came from the act. But then he met a man off the Internet who was sincerely into the scene. It was obvious. The man had quizzed him about his top ticklish areas, and had asked him to rate those spots. All the others in the past had used only their hands to tickle him, but this was different. He was locked, feet extended out of a full-sized stockade; his hands were in fist mitts, joined, and secured to a chain that extended from the ceiling. He was seated on a thin bench, which provided a secure ledge on which to sit, but due to its slim construction, left his ass hanging out. The master returned, and had with him an electric massager. It had been fitted with a long-pronged rubber attachment. Slowly the DOM smoothed oil on the Tony's soles, being careful not to tickle him. The buzz and whine of the massager unit caught Tony's attention, and without a moment more to contemplate what was happening, the massager connect with the ball of his left foot. Ticklish sensations shot through his body with a suddenness and ferocity that pushed the laughter from him. He yanked at his restraints, helpless to protect himself, as the Master moved the massager up and down his sole. Tears formed at the corners of his eyes and he laughed with abandon. He had never felt anything as ticklish in his whole life, and just when he thought he was adjusting to the sensations of the prongs, the Master would use a hairbrush, and then his fingers. It was impossible for Tony to gain control, and he tried with all his might to focus on maintaining control. But it was futile. This DOM knew what he was doing, and the variety of sensations and pressures that he used on Tony made it quite clear their session was going to be a long one, and Tony was truly going

> to be tickled beyond his comprehension. Externally Tony pulled and tried to get away, but internally erotic heat rose from his being, and like the times before, he grew rock hard....

Yes indeed. You are only as good as your tools. Ask any bottom that's tried to have sex with someone less endowed than a male penguin. Tools matter. I have found it's all about experimentation. And tools which work on one person might very well NOT work on another, so when trying things out, don't toss out an item you were sure would have them begging for release which wasn't a stellar reaction. If you think it will work, it probably will. It's just a matter of finding the right guy, the right pressure, and the right area of the body on which to use it. The roster below covers the spectrum – sharp objects, smooth objects, soft things, things with bristles, things with ridges and things with hard edges. The following list are tools I've found to be highly effective from time to time. Most are easily acquirable, and cheap to procure. But a word to the wise… don't use any tool for very long in the same place. Vary your tickling. Change and surprise your ticklee. Using a hairbrush on a guy's sole will definitely get some guys laughing initially. But left to a single sensation, the human brain can shut things down pretty quickly. Tickle them in TWO places, and vary the pressure and location…there's nothing on which to get "focused on" to block.

If you're unsure if you should be using the tool on a submissive…best rule of thumb is to try it out on yourself before you try it on another human!

- **Brushes** – One of my first tickling implements was an artist's paintbrush. I got a wide bristle horsehair brush and remember my glee at seeing how effective it was on a man's soles and bellybutton. It had a little give, but wasn't so soft as to make it indiscernible. There are paintbrushes that have wide heads for painting walls and tiny heads for painting portraits. A good wide bristle hairbrush will often score a home run on the tender ticklish soles of a man. Additionally, the handle end of a paintbrush typically is smooth and polished and when run across the chest or under arms can really be a nice counterpoint to the bristles of a brush. Toilet brushes and tub scrub brushes and even an afro pick can be used as a tickling implement. Be careful not to apply too much pressure when using brushes with stiffer bristles.

- **Toothbrush brushes**- I have an old toothbrush I soak in oil and use to work between toes; it's really quite effective! Electric toothbrushes are great. All are battery powered today – some buzz and some have rotary bristles. The buzzing one's tickle like mad when applied to various areas of the body **Pro Tip... use a buzz toothbrush on the tip of a nose...it will really mess with the submissive.**

- **Combs** – A hair comb run softly up and

down the arch of a man's foot will normally result in at least a laugh. Many ticklers like to take a comb and pull off all the teeth except one in the middle of the comb. And then they use that single plastic tooth to draw on the soles, and to tease between toes. Combs tend to have a sharp feel when used in a sawing motion, so once again, be careful and mindful of the pressure and the application of the comb to skin.

- **Vibrators** – Although most vibrators are designed to be used INSIDE the body, many have variable controls and can be quite effective in the groin, rib and ball area. Keep it moving, and use light pressure. Normally moving the unit in a circle works wonders. Be careful, you don't want to rack your partners testicles, you want to tickle them. So, take care when tickling a man's balls with a vibrating device. External electric massagers normally have a great spiked attachment that is perfect for

feet. Many a submissive has boldly
declared to me that his feet "really
aren't that ticklish", only to have me
break out my massager and oil (as the
DOM in the story did to Tony) and
reduced them to helpless laughter.

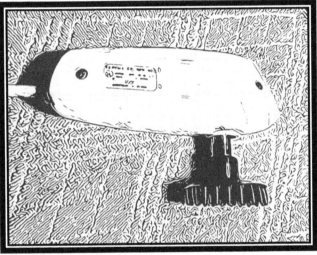

Figure 19 – Massager with Prongs

- **Banjo/Guitar Picks** – Watch any country
  and western singer and you will see a
  hand that resembles something from
  'Nightmare on Elm Street's" Freddy
  Kruger. There are fingertips which the

169

musicians use on their fingers with dull metal points, made for plucking strings on a banjo or guitar. These are perfect for wearing on your hand and then tickling your sub from neck to sole. Use one, use five. The point is it will be a different sensation than your Submissive will ever have experienced on their body. And it will be surprisingly ticklish to them.

Figure 20 – Guitar Finger Picks

- **Writing Utensils** – This is an oldie but goodie. In the early 90's Bob Jones was the only maker for tickling videos, and one of the first tapes of his I witnessed had a tickler using a pen on the soles of a young man. This guy jumped and hollered and laughed hysterically while that pen was being run up and down his soles. The Tickler prompted the captive to tell him what he was writing on the Sub's sole. The Sub, of course couldn't. And the results were hysterical. As a courtesy to your submissive, it's best to use a pen that's run out of ink. If you can't find one, normally oiling up the soles will prevent ink from bleeding onto the skin. Pencils are great on both ends; the lead side or the eraser side. And an old fountain pen also can-do wonders on a man's sole or along his sides.

- **Feathers** – It is highly debated in the tickling community as to whether feathers are effective or not. And in my many years of tickling, I have found a feather or two with the right stiffness to really work well on a neck or ear or between sensitive toes. Feathers which are too soft won't tickle...but they will modify the sensitivity of the submissive during the scene (thus making your next tickle trick on them far more effective.) Don't forget, it's all about keeping your SUB guessing. Often, I like to use a feather under the nose of a submissive. This doesn't tickle but startles them, and makes the NEXT tickle work even better. It's annoying to the submissive, as it prevents them from being able to predict the next tickle. Your local craft supply store has scores of feathers in every size. Go hang out and test them on your arm and face to determine the ones that work best.

- **Tassels** – After I graduated college, I saw my graduation cap and realized I could use a tassel as a tool for tickling a guy. It was very effective and gave me a reason not to toss that old tassel in the garbage. These can be found at fabric supply stores and craft shops.

- **Silk Scarves** – This is another trick for modifying the sensitivity of your tickle submissive. They are light, but have weight. They are soft but can really make your Sub hyper ticklish. After a hard bout of direct tickling, run a silk scarf over their body. I've found using more than one at a time is lots of fun too. Once again, it varies from person to person, and what sends one person into orbit will often not even be noticed by the next. But the secret with scarves is you are tuning your submissive to the sensitivity required to feel it. A few moments with passing a scarf over their body and they will feel the slightest touch. They may not laugh, but they WILL Be stoked for the next tickling trick you use on them. And then watch out!

- **Match Sticks, Tongue Depressors** – A single match stick run up and down the sole of the foot is highly effective, and often used by ticklers to vary the sensation on the foot. Use a brush, then use a match stick, then use a brush again. The SUB has no way of focusing on the sensations. And this is what you want. I like to recycle my used fireplace matches. Also, the tip of a matchstick run lightly over the torso in a squiggly pattern almost always yields a good response. Tongue depressors are great for tickling feet as well, and are easily acquired from your local drug store.

- **String or Shoe Laces** – Cat from www.myfriendsfeet.com uses string or shoelaces between the toes of his men over and over. And you can see the results clearly. The soft skin between the toes is quite ticklish on most men, since there is rarely sensation which stimulates those areas. Running a string between the toes slowly back and forth (like flossing your teeth) really zaps your ticklee. After seeing Cat do this in a few videos, I got the clue and started trying it. It does work very well. And you can vary the kinds of string you use to find the best for your Submissive. Leather boot Laces, cotton athletic shoe laces, packing twine, wax string...even regular floss for teeth work well. Just be careful not to saw back and forth so fast it rope-burns the webbing between the toes.

• **A Riding Crop** – Many DOMs who are into
    spanking own riding crops. These are
    long sticks with a taped handle that are
    outfitted with a loop of leather at the
    end which makes a popping sound
    when used on skin. It has a slight sting
    when used as a paddle on the butt. But
    if used to caress the soles, it can be
    highly erotic and very effective in
    tickling your partner. After tickling your
    Sub for a few moments, pop him with
    the crop on the butt and then return to
    the tickling of his soles, by running the
    leather loop up and down his arch. The
    swing of sensations will keep him
    reeling.

Figure 21 – Riding Crop

- **Medical Nerve Wheel (Wartenberg wheel)**– This device is widely available from numerous Medical supply companies as well as BDSM shops. It is the size of a toothbrush with a circular spiked wheel on its end. This is used by Doctors to check the nerve receptors of the body. When it was used on me, it didn't really tickle, but it did surprise me – enough to make me break down and laugh when the guy playing with me went back to using his hair brush. As with all the tools, this will vary from person to person. Anything is worth a try if it can enhance the experience for you and your sub. Note that this has a slight stinging sensation when run across the body, and a blindfolded submissive can get the false impression they are being cut.

Figure 22 – Wartenberg Wheel

- **ICE** – As you are changing the sensation on your submissive, temperature can be extremely effective. Simply have a glass filled with cubes of ice, take one and trace patterns on your ticklee. Some guys interpret this as a ticklish sensation, some don't. If you don't like holding ice cubes, fill a Paper Cup with water and drop a spoon into it. Put the cup in the freezer and when you are ready to use it, run a bit of hot water over the cup and tug on the handle of the spoon, now frozen in the cup. It will pop right out – instant ice on a stick. When you're done using it, put it right back into the cup while you move on to the next tickle toy.

Figure 23 – Ice on a Spoon

- **Cocktail Fork** – small cocktail forks also can be used to tickle the neck, torso, or soles of the feet and can be super effective. Once again, be mindful of the pressure you use, when applying the device.

- **Bamboo Skewer** – you will be amazed at the response one can get with a little bamboo skewer… lightly use its blunt end to poke and lightly tease soft areas of the belly or on the soles of the feet. And when you're done, you can make kabobs! Easily purchased from any grocery store!

179

- **Metal Chains** – a heavy solid bicycle chain or heavy link chain, when lightly run over a submissive's body can will be a sensation unlike any other, and can surprise them greatly; especially if you've stored it in the freezer before taking it out to use. They won't be expecting it and often being caught off guard will elicit laughter. Your local hardware store will not only have many chains from which to choose, but will also let you cut them to any length you desire (and are extremely cheap!)

- **Oil and Talcum** – covering the body with talcum powder or corn starch or oil will reduce traction on the submissive's skin. Additionally, it will also tend make a person's skin more sensitive. This is a total crap shoot. Some people become 100 times more ticklish with the application of powder or oil, other people don't like the feel of oil on their skin and it can shut them down. Be prepared for either response.

- **Fingernails, Teeth and Tongues**. Oh my. The last items I am listing are the ones most people already embrace. Let your fingernails grow a bit so you can use a single nail to trace a torso, or your whole hand to run a pattern on skin. Alternate tickling a foot with your hands and then running a tongue between toes. Scrape your teeth across a soft sole. This will normally make a guy with ticklish soles just go wild. Lick and prod your way across your SUB's body. In Later sections I will talk about specific target areas for these tongue teases.

Inebriation can also be effective as a method for increasing one's ticklish response. Alcohol and Pot tend to be suppressants, and will induce slumber if used in excess. But a joint will do wonders for increasing the ticklishness of your submissive. As with any substance, make sure you do them responsibly and follow the rules in accordance with your state's laws.

All of these can be highly effective in tickling. And with a number of the items, you can vary which tool you use to make the scene even more effective. It's all about modification of the sensation. Keeping the submissive guessing, and unable to focus on the direct source of the stimulation. Take them from soft touch to rough touch back to soft touch. We will talk more about this in the next chapter!

The Momentum of a Tickling Scene

Jared was spread eagle, affixed to the bed with his hands and legs tied to their respective corners of the head and footboard. He was a giant "X", unable to move more than an inch or two in any direction. He was naked, and Erik had taken care to have Jared pull on the ropes to assure their secureness. It was slightly uncomfortable, knowing he could do absolutely nothing to protect his body from the tickling. Erik approached him, and smiling, begin slowly caressing him. It was practically massage as Erik's fingers lightly drifted around his body. Jared stifled a laugh, grinning as Erik ran a single finger over his bellybutton. "Oh my God" Jared thought to himself, "I'm glad he doesn't realize how ticklish I am there.

" Erik continued the touching. He ran his fingers around Jared's neck and Jared tensed his whole body. Then the fingers trailed back down his body and went to his inner left thigh. Jared moaned and felt his cock stir. This was going to be okay. This tickling thing wasn't that bad. But just as he had that thought, Erik's fingers trailed down to the tops of his feet. They lingered there, gently caressing the toes and the webbing between the toes. A small laugh bubbled from his lips and Erik grinned at the recognition he had found a spot. "Does that tickle, Jared?" he chided. Jared tried to answer but Erik's hand reached up and began tickling his belly button again. Jared jumped; or rather, bounced on the bed as his body reacted and he grew more and more certain this wouldn't be so easy. Erik, continued working his bellybutton until he was laughing nonstop. And then Erik returned to the tops of his feet. It was incredible. Jared had never felt so helpless. And now, it seemed he was far more ticklish than he had first thought. Now, it seemed like he was 10 years old again, being pinned by his brothers and tickled until his mother stopped them. But now…now was …was erotic. No one was going to stop Erik. No. And Erik knew what he was doing, obviously. Suddenly Jared was jarred back to reality as Erik began running his tongue between his toes, while reach up and tickling his inner left thigh with a free hand. Jared dissolved into helpless peals of laughter. Wave after wave overcame him. Erik would tickle, pause to let him almost catch his breath and then move the tickling someplace else. It was maddening. Sometimes he could block it out, but the way Erik moved

185

around his body, varying pressure, speed, and focus made it impossible to get on top of it. This wasn't going to be easy…this WAS going to be hot. And Erik kept moving back to his inner thighs so to top it off, he was now rock hard. The scene progressed and Erik continued plying Jared's body. He'd make quick sharp jabs to his ribs, then tongue his belly button, then tease his ears and neck and then his feet. There was no pattern to it, but the randomness was what was so incredible. He couldn't get used to the sensation like he always had as a child, because Erik never spent more than a few moments in an area. Erik stroked him and tickled him, and stroked him some more. At some point, roughly 45 minutes into the scene he couldn't stop laughing anymore. No matter how hard he wanted he simply couldn't. He saw Erik wiggle his fingers just above his bellybutton, and Jared's laughing increased. "I'm not even touching you," Erik pointed out. Jared couldn't reply. He was too far-gone, and Erik was playing him like a piano. Things proceeded and eventually Erik untied him and flipped him over. He couldn't fight. He couldn't resist. He was a slave to this control and Erik had him. Face down, the sensations were even greater, because he couldn't see or anticipate where Erik was going to tickle him. Just like the start of the session, Erik began by running his fingers lightly over his body. He didn't know what Erik was doing, but whatever it was, it made him ticklish as hell.

Just like running a race, pacing is extremely important when conducting a tickling scene.

Much of experiencing tickling sensations is internal. The submissive reacts to the tickling and the DOM gets excited, pushes the envelope, and then suddenly the submissive isn't ticklish anymore. HUH? He was just ticklish 30 seconds prior, thrashing, begging, and now the exact same action does nothing? What's going on? Well the human being is wired to prevent an overload of sensation. It's something the brain does to allow our bodies to function when under duress. The adrenaline rush allows our body to focus on the most critical component of survival needed at our base level. It's simple. When enduring tickling, the body is put into a stress situation. And at a sustained level, the submissive can eventually gain some control.

Luckily, the mechanism is only hooked to a single nerve bundle; a single area of the body. So, if you work a single area for an extended period of time, it's likely to get "desensitized". To prevent this from occurring, work regions of the body only for short periods of time. Work the torso for 2 to 3 minutes, and then immediately go to the feet, work one foot, then the other. Then move to the stomach. Always spend 2 to 3 minutes max on an area, and then shift. I've found what works best for me is breaking the body into the following regions; Head, Torso, Waist, Legs, and Feet. I move the tickling from region to region. This keeps the SUB from getting attuned. Just as they are beginning to be able to handle the sensations, I switch to another region.

Also, it is very important to map out a submissive's "hot spots". Most experienced ticklers will begin a session by taking a good 10 minutes to <u>lightly</u> touch each region and see what makes the submissive squirm. This isn't about making them laugh. It's about mapping the region like a cartographer. If touch makes them smile or tense at a very very light pressure, you can be sure it's a hot spot. Make a mental note of these places. They are where you should return, if the energy for the scene looks like it's beginning to lose steam. And believe me, it's worth investing the time to catalog these spots. Normally, once you have them identified, they won't change. So, if you tickle the same

Submissive in more than one position, you can normally count on the hot spots to work. Having said that, I will comment many times I've found someone ticklish in a place that had no response the previous time we played. So, every time I play with a tickle sub, I do the hotspot check. And whether ticklish or not, it will drive your submissive absolutely wild with anticipation.

Many times now, I have commented on the pacing and intensity. Tickling is just like massage, in which the receiver has to become accustomed to the person touching them. Most tickling sessions should start with **light touching**. Some of this is to lull your submissive into a false sense of security. It's also to map the hot spots. Additionally, it's also so there's somewhere to go with the scene. As you tickle your submissive, you will see the energy for the scene grows. They laugh harder as they get more tired, or as they lose control more and more. They get more sensitive as the scene progresses. Normally starting with hyper vigilance (as they try to not laugh), diminishing into hypersensitivity.   As soon as you think you have reached a peak in one area of their body, quickly switch to another of the "regions".

In the transition from region to region, don't miss the opportunity to keep the energy moving. Keep your hands in constant contact with the submissive's body. Trail your fingers over their skin as you transition from torso tickling to feet tickling. Letting your fingers graze lightly down the legs. This triggers sensation in your victim. It's critical this energy be connected. Sure, you can simply hop around the bed and poke, prod, and torment in an unconnected fashion. And that certainly can be effective (especially if you're submissive is hooded). But part of the "control" element of the scene is achieved by working the submissive into a state in which they can no longer even conceive of not responding. Getting them so worked up that just the threat of you touching them makes them start giggling. Move the intensity up and down. Take rough tickling and follow it by soft tickling in another region, which you then follow by medium tickling in a hot spot. You will see this technique work even the most mildly ticklish submissive into a frenzy in short time.

Also, as you explore people's body's you will encounter partners who only respond to rough tickling. Some will only respond when it's so soft the normal person could barely feel it. If you try something in an area and it doesn't result in a response, that doesn't necessarily mean that with a different speed and intensity they wouldn't burst out laughing. Gradually increase your pressure and your technique (rubbing verses poking verses licking verses vibration verses hand grabs…) you get the picture.

Ticklish sensations are caused, in a large part, by the sense of surprise. Get your submissive used to a light touch and then vary the tickling with a poke or a scratch from something with an edge. Tease in one area of the body and then tickle their genitalia and then tickle in another region of their body. Don't be afraid to ask them if something tickles. You can even ask them when you start where they are ticklish…and then research their answers.   Find out the pressure and location of the best responses from your submissive. Then use it as a place to return whenever your submissive begins to get used to the sensations in an area (and thus is capable of resisting). There is a rhythm to surprise and with a little practice you will be able to keep them from holding back.

When you have your submissive truly laughing freely, they will typically become a lot more sensitive and at that time you can really push the scene to a form of hysteria. Tickling is like riding a wave, and it has a crescendo. When your submissive is laughing nonstop, watch their breathing. They will laugh and as they inhale and exhale, time your next tickle attack on the exhale. Repeat this action a few times and then pause. Let them take a few breaths and calm down – no more than three full breaths- and tickle on the exhale (don't let them get fully calmed, you'll see them trying to regain some semblance of control). Typically, I'll say "Awe, are you getting control?" and then launch into a full attack on their neck and ribs simultaneously. While they are still laughing, once again time the tickle attack with the exhale.

> **Note: you would be amazed the number of times I get comments from people who claim they cannot get someone to tickle them to excess. Their partners or DOM's simply don't understand the degree of helplessness they seek. And tickling is one of the most non-invasive forms of sexual arousal someone can request. Safe words are used to ensure someone has the ability to express when a limit has been reached, so push the envelope on your Submissives via tickling until you get them to an edge and try to keep them there. You'll be appreciated for sure.**

Also, tickling scenes have an end. Yes, as horrible as it sounds, you have to stop tickling your submissive at some point. You will feel it.

On average, this seems occur around 90 minutes into the session. The energy will drop to an incredibly low level. The Submissive will stop responding and you will also be completely drained. This is typical. Note, this is NOT the same as when sexual climax occurs. Actually, climax should have occurred around 45 minutes into the scene the first time. In the "Lower Body" section, I talk about the impacts of climax on a tickling scene. It's not to be underestimated. I like for my Submissives to cum twice if we have the time. However, when the energy level tanks for you and your partner, this is the cue to change the setting. Tie the submissive in another position. Take a break and get lunch. Do something to break up the activity. You will be amazed at how quickly you and your Submissive can recharge after this exhaustion moment passes.

Face Tickling

The **head** is the main control center of the Submissive.

The face is one of the most sensitive places on the human body. And because of natural "personal space" which humans maintain; it is normally only touched by one's self.   Use this fact to help plot an effective tickle technique for your submissive.   I love to take a feather and use it on the face while I'm tickling another part of the body. I run the feather along the upper bridge of their nose…wiggling it at the base of the nostrils.   The base of the nose at the nostril openings is a very sensitive area, and will always elicit response.   The submissive will normally thrash their head in an attempt to get away from the tease.

Using a feather to tickle the ears can be equally as effective. Run the soft tip of the feather along the opening of the ear. Quickly alternate from ear to ear, once again in an unpredictable fashion.

You can also do this with your index fingers as well. Tickle the inside and just below the ear along the neck. Spider your fingers in a claw-like fashion along the lower edge of the jaw. Barely touch the skin. Truly make this a tease.

The MOST effective tool on the face though, is your tongue. Want to startle your bondage submissive? Use the "Face Licking Trick". In the middle of a tickle session quickly shift to their face and lick their lower jaw line, from chin to eye. Make the lick as wet as possible. And then pop back to tickling them where you were tickling them the moment before. The ludicrousness of the act, coupled by the wet sensation on their face, which they are unable to wipe, will really intensify the tickle.

Another great place to use your tongue is along the eyelid of your submissive. Take a moment to surprise them with it. Kiss them on the mouth, and then kiss your way up their face as part of the moment. When you reach their eyes, they will naturally close them. And then you have them. Run your tongue along their eyelid. Hold their head so as not to allow them to thrash, and then run your tongue softly on the lid of either eye. This act alone will make most people giggle. Combine this licking with tickling somewhere else, and you are sure to produce a laugh. Don't rush this act. Spend a good minute or two licking there. The longer you lick, the crazier they will go. And this is definitely a way to show your submissive who is boss. The feeling of having your eyelid licked is very intense. After a minute, they are feeling like they want to crawl out of their skin. Make it soft. Lick in a line that moves fairly slowly. Back and forth. Trace just below the eyebrows and along the lid. I haven't met a guy yet that wasn't completely blown away by this sensation. And never wipe it off. Just like the "Face Licking Trick", the slightly heightened agitation of that wet eye will keep them disoriented while you are tickling.

The Ear and just below the ear (and slightly to the back of the head) can be a region that will "break" your Tickle submissive; in the sense of them laughing to the point of not being able to resist. Lick the ear from base to top. Nibble the upper edge of the ear. Cover your submissive's ear with your mouth and make a silly repetitive sound. This may seem strange, but do this trick and you will be amazed at the results. Quietly whisper any single sound. Sometimes I emulate a dog's breathing. Making a panting "h" sound that's followed by a wet lick on their ear between pants. The moment the submissive realizes I am emulating a dog, they break. Other times I say "blah-le blah-le blah-le"; this sound forces your tongue out, and so I flick the ear while saying it. Do this while tickling someone's torso simultaneously, and you will get your partner laughing easily.

Under the ear, at the base of the neck (the nape) is perhaps one of the most ticklish places on a man. Especially if licked in a slow, unpredictable pattern. Keep it wet and slippery, and slide your tongue in a circle where the collarbone meets the neck, about 2 inches below the ear. Once again, it's about doing it for more than a moment. Really burrow your head in (to prevent them from shrugging their shoulders to block you from licking there…because they will), and lick. Do it for at least 90 seconds. Run your tongue around that space. You will feel your partner naturally tense as you find the sensitive areas. Obviously hone in and lick them until you've made sure your SUB is happy!

Many Doms use hoods. They are great for making your submissive focus on the sensations they are receiving. With 4 of the 5 senses removed or reduced by a hood (sight, taste, smell, and hearing), the submissive's body is literally forced to amplify the sense of touch. That's the rush of this bondage apparel. And these results make a hood essential for the Dom Tickler. The tickling scene is all about heightening the senses. My favorite hood for tickling is a Lycra hood that is available with a sewn in blindfold. Since its Lycra, it molds to the face, can be easily breathed through, and intensifies touch as well. Put the hood on them without hesitation. It's like a sock, and is easily slipped over a head. Kiss them through the material. Use your mouth on the Lycra. The Submissive will feel it in a very different way. And blinding your tickle partner will make them far more sensitive to erotic energy. Any place you touch, since they can't see it coming, will be a surprise to them. Use this fact to increase the level of the play when the submissive is finally hooded. This is the time to start using one of the brushes or any of the items listed already in the chapter "Tools of the Trade"! They won't know what's coming and the new sensations from those items will be startling.

My favorite tool to use with a hooded submissive is the electric toothbrush on the cheek or at the nape of the neck. It normally produces great results as the ticklee feels a soft whirring/buzzing sensation which they cannot identify. Like the feather, running this along the upper lip (at the base of the nose) through the hood is also very fun, and will produce positive results! I like to use an electric toothbrush on the very tip of a Submissive's nose; try it and watch the great response. Yes, your submissive will HATE it, but don't let up – annoy the hell out of them and then tickle them in another region.

A particularly devious method of tickling a submissive is to order them to open their mouth wide, or use a ring gag to force their mouth open. Then wet your index finger, reach in and rub the upper roof of their mouth. This can be a maddening sensation for your submissive, and they will declare you a Dom God for having the know how to tease them like no other has! Watch their response and threaten to do it again, unless they comply to some demand. I promise this will coerce them!

As a few of the descriptions have indicated, the techniques are far better in combination with tickling in other regions simultaneously. Why? Well the face is what we pay attention to <u>first</u>. And if you are teasing someone's neck, they'll have no resistance when you add a rib tickle.   When a tickling scene begins to rise in intensity, these are the tricks you can use to ensure you keep the scene moving along an edge. Ergo the term "Edge play".

These are components which maneuver your submissive into losing control. Sure, they will give in to the tickling as part of their loyalty to serving their Dom in the best manner the Dom sees fit, but when they begin to reach a point of helplessness, that's when the edge is achieved.

Arm and Torso Tickling

9 out of 10 men will squeal when surprised by a poked in the ribs! This region of the body is filled with sensitive areas which are typically not touched by others very often.

Starting with the hands, the center of the palm when lightly tickled can be maddening. I once saw a submissive tied down and his Dom had tied rope around each finger, and then literally tied his hands open. Then the Dom used the quill of a feather to trace patterns on his captive's palms. The Submissive was completely blown away by the sensations. As you are doing this, combine it with light tickling on the lower forearm. The lower region on a man's arm where no hair grows is extremely ticklish, so use a fingertip to trace that smooth area, or a tongue.   These sensations sometimes aren't enough to elicit a laugh, but they will work to sensitize your tickle bottom, which is ultimately the goal.

From elbow to armpit, a number of muscles

and nerves intersect. The best way to work this area is to take your hand and trace light patterns in the hollow of the armpit. Make the tickling just hard enough for them to feel it, but not so pressure intensive to leave indentations in the skin. You will see your Sub tense their body as these sensations overwhelm them. It's at this moment you should change the sensation to a light jab. Do this three to four times and then return to the light tickling. Try spidering your fingers from the armpit to the chest area, working the lower edge of the Pectoral muscles (just along the edge of the nipple area).   And when your partner begins to tense, jab them (lightly) again in the pit area.   And then, before your partner adjusts to the feel of your fingers, lower your tongue and run it from their nipple to the armpit.

Pro tip: I always tell my subs to be sure not to wear deodorant when they come to play. This way I can bury my tongue in the hollow of their armpit and lick to my heart's content. There is nothing worse than a mouth full aluminum sulfide, to bring me back to the harsh reality that I forgot to mention this to my bottom.

I find tongue licking in the armpit in a circular fashion, will make most sensitive guys break down with laughter. And be patient. Guys will try and stave off the sensations, and might succeed for a few moments. But if you feel their body tense, you know you have found a hotspot. A little persistence and you will be rewarded with peals of laughter.

Also, at the base of the armpit "hollow", aligned with the nipple, is a soft sensitive area, which is typically a hotspot. It's so sensitive that simply holding your hand there will fill your submissive with dread and anticipation. A slight unexpected flutter of the fingers will typically send them off the charts. It's a soft subtle move, but highly effective.

Twice in my life I have tickled guys to the point of losing bladder control and both of them were made to finally break by tickling them on the soft sensitive area that runs between the elbow and the armpit, along the bicep. It's an area most people aren't touched and once you have a submissive to the hypersensitive state, can truly take the ticklee to new depths of ticklishness.

A whole book could be written on nipples. They are extremely sensitive on most men, and run the gamut from ticklish to erotic. Either way you win, but it's worth taking the time to explore their sensitivity. Early on in the session, when I am mapping out hot spots, I test the nipples. First, I use my fingers. Take the thumb and forefinger with a twisting motion and brush the nipple; like turning the dial on a radio. I continue to tweak them watching for a response. Gradually I try different pressures until I find the one that works best. Place your mouth over their nipple and flick your tongue along the nipple head. The quicker you flick your tongue, the more intense the sensation will be.   When this is combined with tickling the armpit, or upper arm region, I find the response fairly effective. Nipples can bring great response from your sub – use brushes along the head of the nipple, or use an electric toothbrush – vary the pressure and pattern and you are bound to find one of them either hits your submissive with erotic energy or ticklish sensations.

And as the chapter opening indicates, getting my Submissive to giggling is normally achieved in short form with the upper body. It's rare I meet someone who isn't ticklish on their ribs. The torso is a minefield of ticklish explosions waiting to fire. Take your hands and lightly kneed the area within the ribcage. Pulse your tickling in three quick attacks (Three-Pulse). If your Sub laughs, pulse it again, three times, and pause. Do both sides of the rib cage at the same time. Working up from the lower rib to the armpit. Often, I will make a game of tickling my submissive in this fashion. Once the scene has heated up and my tickle bottom is laughing freely, I ask them "how many ribs do you have" and then start tickling my way up their ribs counting. For each number, I do the three-pulse tickling. When they laugh hysterically and thrash, I say "Oh man, you made me lose count," and I begin again at their lowest rib, going back to "one".

Remember each person you tickle will be

different. Many submissives don't respond to tickling through grabbing and pokes, but will respond to a rub… use your hands, holding your first and second finger together and lightly move your hand on their torso in a rubbing fashion. Plant your fingers on their body and make a waving motion over their skin. Slide your hand a few inches and rub again. Repeat this in small increments. Increase the pressure or the speed of the wave as you tease and tickle your submissive.

Another trick for rib tickling is to ask the submissive which tickles more "HERE" (grab their lowest rib) or "HERE" (grab their upper most rib). Regardless of the answer they give, tell them you don't believe them, and then test it again.   Use this trick on any two parts of the body to keep your victim reeling.

There is a line that extends from the inner armpit to the groin area along the side of the torso which can be quite effective to light touches. Take your fingers and run them up and down your SUB's side. Keep it light and continue the motion up and down. When you feel them begin to break into laughter, add a three-pulse grabbing on the ribs. Additionally, you can use your Index finger and thumb in a pinching fashion, pinching up and down the sides of the torso. Be sure to make it light…too much pressure and it will turn into a painful experience; not part of this scene at all!

Lastly, the waist is truly a hotspot on 99.99999 % of the subs I have tickled. The band of flesh from bellybutton to upper groin can always be counted as a place to send guys into hysterics. I normally use my mouth and lick in a circle in an area just below the belly button aligned with either nipple. Basically, just above the hip joint on the lower stomach. Lick and kiss that area while adding a simultaneous three-pulse tickle to the ribs. This always gets them laughing, and cannot be suppressed by a ticklish guy from my experience.   Many a man has told me he isn't ticklish and once he is restrained and helpless, I will dive in and start licking this area. The response is immediate and debilitating to them every time. Once they get laughing, move your licking to a soft bite/kiss and nip everywhere in that region with your mouth. The key with this move is to simultaneously tickle them elsewhere at the same time. Try it. You'll be pleased with how effective this will be.

Many times, a session will get to an escalated level and the bottom needs to breathe. I will give them a moment to catch their breath, and then lower my mouth to the waist area and start to lick in a circle. Having done this to them earlier, they are expecting the three-pulse at the same time, and will tense for it. It's far more intense to have them expect it. I just keep licking their upper waist and most times, they begin laughing freely without the pulse. Once they have broken down and started laughing again, then add the three-pulse, which will catch them off guard, and push the intensity back to where it was when you stopped!

The same area in which you are licking can also be tickled with a squeezing motion, using your hand. Form a "C" with your hand, cupping your four fingers together and separating your thumb. Place your hand so the open part of the "C" encircles their waist area, fingers towards their back, thumb on top, and give a light squeeze. Move your hand up and down lightly gripping that area. Grip and squeeze from the hips up to just below the ribs on the sides of the torso. A little practice and you will be able to move the scene to laughter in short order.

Tickling the Lower Body

"Where am I ticklish? My balls...why?"

Often when meeting people in a bar, as part of the pickup I will point-blank ask them where they are ticklish. The average smart-ass answer tends to be "my balls", and although it's hardly a surprise when a guy says "his balls", I always know that if I do end up tying and tickling them, there is going to turn out to be many more places besides the testicles that will tickle before it's all over.

As many know from sex, the groin is a highly sensitive area. But for tickling there are a few spots which are more effective.   Where the leg meets the hip there is a soft crease of flesh. This crease is very ticklish on most men, and I've found the best method for tickling it is either by licking in a circle in that area, or by using the tip of your thumb and wiggling it softly along the crease. Normally it's best to save this for later in the session, once it has heated up and your submissive is highly reactive. In the few sessions in which someone lost control of their bladder and pissed himself, this was the area that helped bring it on (in addition to upper arm tickling). You'll tell if it's a hotspot immediately, as the man will literally yelp with laughter and thrash.

The balls and the taint (the soft skin between the base of the balls and the asshole) are definitely good areas to tease. Using an electric toothbrush on the taint will normally produce decent results, and if you've had your submissive shave their balls (which I highly suggest) then using fingers, tongue, hair brush, feather or electric toothbrush will be quite effective on them. I rarely find that tickling the balls alone will bring laughter, but you can combine it with Torso or neck tickling for much better results.

Also, along the top of the thigh, from hip to knee can be highly effective. Use your hands in a spidering motion up and down the thigh. As a kid, there was a game called "Horses eating corn" in which someone would grab just above the knee using the "C" hand (described in the previous chapter) and lightly squeezing twice. If there were no response, they'd move the hand up the thigh toward the groin by an inch and repeat the move. It was a quick thing that was a surprise. After three or four moves up the thigh, normally your victim would cry out in laughter and pull away. Don't underestimate this method. It's startling, and after being tickled in another region, can be a great way to move the energy to the lower body, and change the level of sensitivity.

The inside of the leg, where the leg meets the butt is also a hot spot on many men. Reach in-between your Submissive's legs from the front, fingers curving underneath them, thumb to the side of the balls and wiggle your fingers. Don't dig in, and be sure not to grip too tightly. The object here is to flutter your fingers and set that sensitive area at their butt on fire.   Roughly 70% of all guys will begin laughing uncontrollably (based on the last 10 guys I tickled!) This is another of those spots if you save for a surprise tickle after working another of their body zones, will produce desired results.

> Pro tip: I would be remiss if I didn't mention a spot that has brought many of my men to climax when combined with jacking. On the inside of the leg, just above the knee is an area that when licked brings arousal. The sensations are enough that if you jack your submissive until they approach orgasm, adding licking to this area will bring them off. I've done this countless times, and although it's not really a point of tickling, perhaps I can help you make your next JO session far more exciting! Jacking a man while tickling them is often very effective (but typically will get them to orgasm, so pay attention to your submissive).

Be sure to test your SUB's kneecaps when you are working their lower body. Lightly tickle their kneecap, alternating your fingers in a quick fashion over and around their knee. At the same time, take nips from just below their kneecap with your mouth. Be careful – many men will buck and thrash and, yes, jerk their knee. This can be quite painful to you as your teeth get jammed, and to your submissive as your teeth go into their knee (this alone is justification for bondage during a tickling scene!)   Also try running your fingers over the soft skin on the back of their knees; if your submissive is tied face down, then lick that area. Take your electric toothbrush and run it over the kneecap in a circular fashion. Simultaneously, lick and nip just above the kneecap of the same leg. Then, roll that toothbrush to behind the knee while continuing the mouth on kneecap action. If it's done correctly, you will get a good laugh!

The one most surprisingly ticklish place on many people's lower body has got to be the shins. It's one of those areas that unless you have experience tickling multiple guys and have really taken your time to explore a ticklish man's body, you might never find. Try light tickling with your fingers, or run an electric toothbrush along the line from just below the knee to the ankles on the top side of the leg. Go slowly, and trace a long line back and forth along that area! I love waiting until I have blindfolded or hooded my Sub, and then I work their inner thigh while running my other hand over their shins. This works like a champ at prodding the laughter from them.

If your submissive is face down, you'll have

access to their butt and asshole and don't underestimate the sensitivity of this region as well. An electric toothbrush used on upper globe cheeks of someone's ass can produce raucous laughter in some. Additionally, you can use a feather or fingertips along the crack of the ass and over the asshole to surprise and tickle many. For those inclined, rimming/licking this area can bring erotic energy to the play, which when combined with touching / tickling another region to be quite a ticklish situation.

Lastly, I need to mention, "polishing the apple".   This is a term used for continuing to jack a man's penis after he has achieved orgasm.

Yes, after a man cums he is the ***most sensitive*** and as a Dom tickler it is your job to keep this fact secret until after you have brought your Submissive to climax. You've spent 90 minutes exploring their body, working their energy levels up and down, and if you're good, you have probably been manipulating and stimulating their cock. While you are teasing them, try the "PALM-ROLL". Lick your palm and get it extremely wet. Then open your hand and place it on the top of his dick on the head. Roll your palm in a counter-clockwise fashion with firm pressure. Your submissive will be flooded with extremely intense sensations. Sometimes they say they feel like they are going to piss. Don't worry…they won't for a while, it's just the result of this kind of stimulation. Careful with the PALM-ROLL. It is so intense that it often brings men to climax very quickly. Be ready for that kind of response. If you feel the submissive tense in preparation to climaxing, immediately switch to tickling their torso or feet, and move that energy from their climax to those spots. It will effectively back off your submissive. In this manner you can keep your tickle sub on the edge of climax for a very long time. Get them close to climaxing, and then tickle them just before they can release. Repeat this over and over. And when they finally do climax, it will have an intensity they might not have experienced before. Be sure to remember this technique when he finally cums; because at that point, his whole body is going to become one giant nerve ending. Even the most non-ticklish guys are extremely ticklish after climaxing. Sometimes it's only for a few moments; sometimes the effects last for a while. Climaxing takes a great deal of energy from the shooter. At that moment the submissive will be more ticklish than at any other time. Use that fact. Don't allow the refraction period to be wasted. Continue jacking them after they have cum, and with your other hand, tickle their body. Jump zone to zone tickling their torso, then their feet, then their neck; all the while continuing the stimulation to their cock. Use the Palm Roll and really see them be hit with a wave of energy! Tickle your submissive through the orgasm and into their next. Many men get hard almost immediately afterward, if the tickling continues. If you are into milking, this is your entry point to building the next climax.

Remember your tickle submissive has a safe word to stop the action if things get too "over-the-top", so don't be afraid to push the envelope a little.

Tickling the Feet

"Fuck fuck fuck fuck fuck. I knew I should never have agreed to this. He said he'd leave my fuckin' feet alone. He swore he wouldn't...ooo ooohhho ahhhahah hahahaha hahha....no ...hahahahaha". The Sub's thoughts raced as his body responded to the tickling.

The master had finished untying the Sub's shoes, throwing them to the ground, and had taken his fingers and started stroking along the Sub's soles. Up and down. Up and down. And the Sub, who was tied on a ladder suspended between two hobbyhorses, was doing his best to maintain composure, but the master continued to work his feet. His legs filled with tension, and his feet started to twitch in avoidance of the master's fingers. But they were deft.

Rope encircled his body at each rung, and the master had already cut away his shirt and his pants. Only his shoes and socks had remained on, as they had agreed. But a moment ago he had lashed out at the master, calling him "a worthless loser". And the master's response was quick and precise; the shoes came off and his soles were now being worked over. The ticklish sensations were beyond tolerable, and the Sub dissolved into helpless laughter. Just as the master knew would happen.

It wasn't long before the socks came off and the master really started to focus on the feet. He traced long fingernail patterns along the bottom of the Sub's foot. And being so far away from the head, the Sub had no way to see what the master was doing, or even to which foot he was focused. The chuckles and giggles became hearty laughter with a slightly higher pitch. Somehow giving over and laughing brought a floodgate of sensitivity rushing through his psyche. Yanking him to a place within. His body was being played, and his own body is what was responsible for this ruthless response. His laughter made him more sensitive and the pace of the scene increased as the master licked and sucked the toes of each bare foot.

The Sub hardly noticed as the master pulled a bottle of talcum from his bag and sprinkled it on the toes of the Sub's left foot. All he knew was suddenly the man's fingers were silky and slippery as they glided along his soles, and there was no holding back. No, no holding back or cognizant control. His body tensed, but still could not avert the sensations that flooded him. The master paused the action, allowing the submissive to catch his breath, and retrieved another bottle from a bag. It contained massage oil, which was spread on the Sub's right foot. The master reached into the bag again, and feeling the item for which, he was searching, exclaimed "ah, here it is!" The master held up the hairbrush and asked the Sub in a clear, firm voice "Worthless loser? Was that what you said?" He lowered the brush to the oiled sole. The Sub laughed harder, and gave over to the sensations. His feet destroyed *him, and now there was no escape. He was controlled and dominated by the man who had broken his promise. But it was the hottest fucking sex he had ever had. And it was only getting better. His cock was rigid and ready for whatever was about to happen next. Damn this was hot...*

Okay, I'll start here by saying in the above story, we have a master who breaks a promise to his submissive. Let me say we assume this wasn't a limit, because the Sub didn't use a safeword and end it. Will the Dominant partner get to play with this submissive again? Probably not, but that is between them. I feel the need to clarify this, as I don't want to be accused of suggesting breaking promises to a helpless submissive is appropriate action. However, if a Sub decides to shout insults at me when I have them tied… I might very well tickle the shit out of them in the most merciless way possible. And typically, if a guy's feet are ticklish, it's going to be maddeningly agonizing and effective to fuck with their feet. But then – I'd never play with someone who said tickling was a limit, because it's important to me for that to be part of a scene.

Start _light_ with the feet. Use feathers and fingertips when you first are mapping out hot spots on your submissive. Typically, ticklish areas on the foot are as follows:

- Tops of the feet
- Between the toes
- The tips of the toes
- The Ball of the foot, and the Achilles heel
- The Arch of the foot
- At the base of the third and fourth toe

Sounds like basically the whole foot, right? There are a number of nerve bundles that all come together around and along the feet. Use light pressure initially, until you have determined the right pressure to use. Some people will begin to laugh with just simple light movement along the feet. Others aren't ticklish on their feet at all until after they have become hypersensitive. Others aren't ticklish even a little until you use an electric toothbrush or a scrub brush on the feet. It's gonna take some experimentation, and timing. Take your time. Watch how your submissive responds.

Lube/baby oil/massage oil along the feet will make them slippery and will heighten the sensitivity. Be careful, as some people immediately get turned off with the feeling of oil. However, the use of oil is critical when using a hairbrush on someone's soles, as you want to make sure friction doesn't hurt them. Talc powder can result in the same smoothing effect. Spread the oil liberally and continue to add more oil as you play.

I like to take a shoelace and run it between the toes. Same with a feather. This is a very very sensitive area of the feet...and licking there can also be effective to get your submissive laughing.

There is a fellow on the internet who is into extreme tickling and will heat the soles of the feet with hand held hair dryers and heat lamps before tickling. It appears to be very effective at making the Submissive's feet become highly sensitive. However, this could just as easily burn someone, so please be careful if you choose to warm the soles of someone's feet.

I've found an effective way to tickle toes is to hold the foot from the top, thumb on one side of the foot, fingers on the other, and then use a hairbrush in an up and down fashion over the sole of the foot from heel to toes and back. This up and down motion tends to tickle the hell out of a bound guy.

An electric toothbrush along the tips of the toes can also be very ticklish to a bound submissive.

Where to find the Tickle Tribe

With the advent of the INTERNET so many outlets have emerged to support any and all fetish play. In the beginning of the book I discussed I am not a spokesperson for the Tickling Community. I do not represent nor endorse any of the resources I am about to list, however I'm listing them in a spirit of fellowship and support. Your experiences with them may be good or bad. Remember that many of the online fetish communities are open forums. People of ALL ages (that's right, even minors) and creeds, and colors contribute to the dialog. No one really is a referee and there are Lurkers and Trolls (people whose sole purpose in life is to criticize or try and find fault) with everything they read.   Approach these resources at your own risk.

A few common terms used in the tickling
community:

> **Tickler** – The person doing the tickling
>
> **Ticklee** – The person getting tickled
>
> **A Switch** – A person who does both

Also, websites come and go like the wind –
my apologies if you reach out to one of these
resources only to find it no longer exists.

Sites for Tickle Discussions

DISCUSSION boards – The following websites have forums that cross a myriad of topics related to tickling. They always include a membership of some kind; typically, free. They normally have forums where people can post questions, and others can post answers to the questions. And they tend to be organized by topics. I am ERIK11 on all of these boards, if you'd like to exchange messages with me!

- **www.tklfrat.com** – This site has been around for over a decade, and not only has forums for discussion but hosts an annual male on male Ticklefest which is managed by the membership and attended by people from all over the world. The annual gathering is a holdover from the old MTMTN (Man to Man Tickle

Network) which used to hold annual gatherings before the advent of the internet. When TKLFRAT formed, the group migrated to this site and has used it ever since. It has stories, and links to video clips people have found. This is a free website. It supports public and private messaging between members.

- www.ticklemediaforum.com – This is a Pan Sexual website devoted to tickling. Note that it primarily services the straight community and every 5 or 6 posts about Male on Male tickling garners a TROLL comment about it being "gross". Regardless, it is a great resource if you are looking for announcements about new video clips, or leads on tickle parties that are going on. For the most part the site is friendly and nonjudgmental. In addition to public forms, it supports private messages between members.

* www.fetlife.com – This site has been around for many years and caters to fetish players of any and all types. It is pan sexual, and has as many gay groups as str8 groups. You can catch announcements about upcoming tickle events and find others that share an interest in tickling. This site works at being all things to all fetishists – unfortunately, in my opinion, it's what makes it hardest to use. It's rare to find quick communication or anyone seeking to actually meet (although many will fantasy chat with you via the conversation forums for years). For a subscription fee you can view any of the thousands of amateur video clips others have uploaded to share. It supports exchanging messages

between members (paying and nonpaying).

- **www.recon.com** – Technically this last one isn't a discussion board, as it has no forums for posting questions – this is my all-time favorite men for men community site. It's a shared interface between about 10 other fetish websites and is specifically designed to locate gay people from the fetish community to chat with and meet. There are no forums, only lists of people nearby and far away. It has extensive searching, gallery sharing and messaging. When people ask how I meet other guys into bondage – it's this site to which I always refer. My profile is *www.recon.com/erik11*   Hit me up sometime there and let me know how you liked the book!

A Tip About Anonymous Connects

When dealing with anonymous connects (strangers from the Internet or a bar, or a dungeon), many times I hear, "How do I know you won't chop me up into little pieces once I'm tied?" I often joke that I'd never do that until the third or fourth session, when they really trusted me, but it truly is an honest question to a real concern. After I'm done joking, I offer a simple solution. I give them MY phone number and have them call me from their phone. My phone doesn't allow anonymous phone calls, and although I don't mention this, this also provides a certain sense of security for me as well. I explain to the Submissive that if I was going to do anything illicit, I wouldn't want there to be a legal, public record connecting us. I'd want there to be NO record between us, like an anonymous pick up in a bar. I tell them I won't play unless they DO call me (and it's true...anyone that refuses to call me must be hiding something.) This almost always assuages them. A few times people will say...okay, but I'd still be dead. I have no answer for them, and normally these are people that aren't sincere about playing. If someone is sincere, and is willing to take a few steps to insure their own safety you can bet they are interested. If you provide a simple solution to something that weighs heavy on the mind you establish trust! And that is the most important thing to getting your submissive tied down. What do I do with phone numbers on my caller id? I write them down. Should someone forget something, or something ends up stolen (yes, unscrupulous types will gladly rob from you the moment the scene is over and you excuse yourself for a bathroom break), you have somewhere to go with it. Additionally, if it's a new friend, you have a way to re-invite them in the future, should you desire.

Do NOT agree to have a stranger to your place without taking some steps to protect yourself. And news flash – just because you're a tough Dom, doesn't mean someone couldn't bring a gun, tie you up with your OWN secure equipment, rob you and leave you to your own devices. They would have asked if you live alone and been very interested in your secluded hacienda of love. Perfect to take advantage of the unsuspecting – and who more unsuspecting than a guy that thinks he is going to be dominating another. Imagine they don't arrive alone, bring a friend, and then you have two unknown people in your home. An ounce of prevention will make a huge difference. Make sure you have a way to find these people you allow into your private space once they vanish!

Video Clip Sites

CLIP Sites are websites which provide clips on a regular basis to their paying members. There are many and I will do my best to provide information about all of them of which I'm aware. Each provide a mechanism to watch clips or to download clips for later viewing. Typically, these sites provide little else other than clips, however where this departs, I'll note in the following list.

Tickling clips are often named in a manner to indicate the kind of tickling you will see in the media. Either in the clip title, or the clip description, you are likely to see following classifications:

M/M – indicates Man Tickling Man
M/F – indicates Man Tickling Female
F/M – indicates Female Tickling Male
F/F – indicates Female Tickling Female

- www.myfriendsfeet.com – This member only site is one of the true gems of the tickling community, focusing primarily on Male on Male tickling and foot fetish enthusiasts. For a small monthly fee, you get weekly tickle clips and weekly foot fetish clips. They feature men of many types and ages, young and old, body builder model to guy off the street. They have clips which are story related, as well as simply fetish play. They also offer fetish fiction stories written by site contributors (I wrote for them for a while, many years ago). Recently they also purchased the Jason Strong tickling website content, and they offer the Jason Strong clips to their members. Additionally, they also offer members free access to tickle fetish illustrated images from another partner site "Achilles Heel Art". By far, they are the best tickle/foot fetish website around, and have continued to grow and nurture their holdings and offerings.

- www.psmtickling.com – This website was originally created in Rome, but now resides out of Barcelona Spain. They sporadically post tickling clips for purchase via the clips4sale.com site (see reference to this site at the end of this list). They regularly participate in pansexual fetish gatherings, and sell the videos of these random men being tied and tickled. Additionally, they have story-based clips and clips devoted solely to tickling. Their clips include bondage and genuinely ticklish guys.

- www.ticklishlads.com – This British based company has done a number of tickle clip sites. They have a monthly fee which provides access to a plethora of their foot fetish/tickling clips. They typically use European twink type (early 20's) models often interacting with each other, and are exclusively a male on male tickle site. If you like younger guys being tickled, this might be the site to check out.

- www.tickledhard.com – This is one of the first online membership clip sites to focus primarily on orgasm and tickling combined. If you like seeing men tied down, tickled and brought to orgasm and then tickled some more, this is the site for you. The clips are posted regularly and there is a monthly fee for membership. The models vary in age and size, but all are ticklish and all are brought to orgasm as part of the scenes. These clips tend to be high intensity, and the ticklees are always highly reactive.

- www.menonedge.com – This is one of a score of websites owned by Kink Video. These are typically story based, and are always top-notch quality from a production and model perspective. Men on Edge is about edge play, and in all of them, the models are put into a number of bondage positions, brought close to orgasm, teased, tickled, teased more, and ultimately brought to climax. They aren't tickling videos, but many include some tickling here and there. There is a monthly fee, and clips are posted on a regular basis. I should note that kink.com offers many straight and gay themed porn sites – all high quality and all great in their own special way.

- www.bondagejeopardy.com – I worked with this company to produce three different videos: "Lights Out", "Tickle Training", and "Breaking in". All videos are story based, often involve kidnapping of some sort, and always include men who are gagged as part of the scene. Imagine "The Hardy Boys" except when they are tied up, they are in their underwear. There is rarely an orgasm in these clips, but they are always interesting. Often, they circle around a competition, whose losers are tied and tickled by the winners. It's about as soft porn as you can get. Eventually, they split into their sister site *TickleJeopardy.com*. They have a monthly fee, and their clips are posted on a regular basis.

- www.ticklingmalefeetasyoulike.com – This site is primarily focused on Latin men, is a pay site and posts clips regularly. Most of the clips are simple bondage and tickling. Sometimes the subjects are masked or in super hero masks. Often the tickler is not seen. Overall, I liked this site for its basic production values and the great ticklees they use.

- www.bubbafeet.com – This is a FREE site. According to their main page: "There is no sex. No nudity. No suggestive poses. Just real-life blue-collar men and their boots, socks and feet with some tickling thrown in."   If you are looking for rough non-model type guys, this might be your thing. If you like construction workers tied down and teased, this site would be right up your alley.

- www.tickleabuse.com – This site has evolved into my second favorite clip site over the years. They feature lots of great female tickling male, as well as male tickling male video clips. They charge a monthly fee, and produce clips…when they feel like it. I say this because twice I've joined their site, only to have them post zero male related tickling for 6 weeks at a time. Overall, they do produce great videos, often include orgasm, and the models are genuinely ticklish.

- www.clips4sale.com – And lastly is the granddaddy of all the fetish clip sites. It should be noted that 95% of the sites I mention sell their most popular clips through this central hub of fetish material. There is no cost for access to this site. You can select any of thousands of fetish topics from sex with bubbles to mud wrestling midgets. A good search of "TICKLING" or "TICKLING MALE" or "TICKLING HAIRY" or "TICKLING HANDJOBS" will result in tons of stores which will offer to sell you a clip at whatever price they think fair. Because this site is a clearing house, it's constantly updated. Most sites will show you a GIF or a small preview clip so you can determine if you like the players and the presentation. They also graciously provide a 90-day restoration service should you accidentally lose clips you' ve purchased from them.

Gatherings

Throughout the year there are parties held around the world involving tickle play. These parties are hosted, and often require an entrance fee. I'm going to list the ones I've attended in the past, and suggest as you learn and maneuver the various discussion websites I mentioned, you will see advertising posted for them. I encourage you to go! This is the best way to meet other people that share your interest in tickling/fetish/whatever.

www.FootMenNYC.com – If you are in New York City, or any of the surrounding areas, this is the resource for you! This group has been around for over a decade, and their gatherings are top notch and always sold out. They advertise themselves as *"Private, Social, Friendly, Supportive, Playful, Network-y Parties in NYC – For Men into Men's Feet, Footwear, and Tickling"*. They have an international mailing list / roster with over 3000 members and send out periodic notification emails to those who opt to provide their email address. Additionally, they post announcements on www.fetlife.com and www.tklfrat.com. I have been to many of their parties and never had a bad time. And I honestly made friends through them that I'd otherwise never have met. <u>Not to be missed</u>.

Ticklefest -This festival is definitely the oldest reoccurring gathering of tickle fetishists in America, and one of the highest attended Male on Male tickling events in existence. The location varies from year to year. The last one was in Anaheim California and the 2019 festival is currently slated to be in Las Vegas. Attendees typically hang out, have tickle demonstrations, and typically there is a dinner. There is a broad spectrum of ages and personalities that attend this annual gathering, and in general, the attendees are friendly and inviting. This is always advertised on TKLFRAT.COM, FACEBOOK, and FETLIFE.COM and every year there is a new site website devoted to the event.

Erik11 Tickle Parties in Austin Texas – Get to know me, and I'll invite you to one. No one is invited that hasn't played with me one on one first. Want to know what goes on? Read my section on how to throw a Tickle Party!

New Year's Foot Ball – This was another New York event, and one of the best foot fetish/tickling events at its time. There hasn't been one for a while, and maybe someday there will be another. It was held in a giant warehouse, and people from the foot fetish and tickling community came together to ring in the new year.

In addition to gatherings specifically targeting tickling, there is a wealth of contact to be made with the fetish community in general. In my experience, about 50% of all submissives into bondage enjoy tickling. Think about that. If you are seeking a playmate for tickling, and you know bondage will be involved, why limit your search to those that explicitly declare tickling as an interest? Why not look for anyone into bondage and then bring up tickling? Same with Sub/Dom play. If a submissive will do whatever a master wants (within limits), then why only seek for tickling.

Seek submissives and explore tickling. These kinds of people will be far more likely to agree to trying it, than someone with zero fetish experience that's intimidated by just a picture of handcuffs. Don't limit yourself, and don't treat your sexuality like a dirty little secret. Lead with what you want, and most of the time…you'll end up getting it.

Here is a list of Gay fetish-oriented gatherings at which I've met and played with tickle partners.

- **CLAW** (Cleveland Leather Awareness Week) - This is held at the end of April in Cleveland Ohio. This gathering boasts over 100 free classes (once you pay for registration), fills 4 downtown hotels in Cleveland, and includes a dungeon space and bathhouse as part of the package. I loved this gathering, because it wasn't about a competition, and the classes were done professionally, and even included surveys at the end. In 2019 I'm teaching "The Dom's Guide to Tickling" at this event.

- **DORE Alley (Up your alley festival)** – is

always held the last Sunday of July in San Francisco. This is a gay event, and once again, its fetish aligned.

- Folsom Street Festival – Held annually at the end of September in San Francisco, this pan sexual festival brings thousands of men and women into everything from BDSM to COSPLAY. There are always play parties and events and someone into tickling will probably find someone that shares their interest. I had an amazing scene once at the Sanctuary play space with a guy I met at the festival.

- IML (International Mister Leather) – is held over Memorial Day weekend in Chicago. This is a gay event and is completely fetish aligned. Typically boasts attendance of 10,000 or more people.

- MAL (Mid Atlantic Leather) - is held the third weekend in January in Washington DC. This is a gay event and is completely fetish aligned. Typically boasts attendance of 5,000 or more people.